Designing
Instructional
Text

Designing Instructional Text

Third Edition

James Hartley

 **NP**

Kogan Page Ltd, London
Nichols Publishing Company,
New Jersey

First published in 1978 by Kogan Page
Second edition published in 1985 by Kogan Page
This third edition published in 1994 by Kogan Page

Kogan Page Limited
120 Pentonville Rod
London N1 9JN

British Library Cataloguing in Publication Data

A CIP record for this book is available from the British Library.

ISBN 0 7494 1037 X

This third edition published in the USA in 1994 by
Nichols Publishing, PO Box 6036, East Brunswick, New Jersey 08816

Library of Congress Cataloging-in-Publication Data

Hartley, James, Ph. D
    Designing instructional text/James Hartley.—3rd ed.
        p.   cm.
    Includes bibliographical references and index.
    ISBN 0 89397 399 8 (Nichols) : $33.95
        1. Textbooks–Authorship.   2. Teaching–Aids and devices.
    3. Printing, Practical–Style manuals.   I. Title.
    LB3045.5.H37   1994   94-5966
                                                                  CIP

Typeset by DP Photosetting, Aylesbury, Bucks
Printed and bound in Great Britain by
Biddles Ltd, Guildford and King's Lynn

Contents

Preface to the third edition

Designing Instructional Text is intended to give general guidelines for the producers of instructional materials. These guidelines are based upon current practice and upon a critical reading of relevant research.

The notion of planning the layout of such text in advance is emphasized throughout the book. This is done for two reasons. First, instructional text is usually more complex in its structure and appearance than is continuous prose – and thus it requires greater thought about its presentation. Second, technical advances in print and publishing mean that more and more non-specialists are now involved. Planning can help such people to be more effective.

Many people producing instructional materials today use computer-aided means to do so. However, the aims of the first five chapters in the book are to outline the relevant thinking behind earlier traditional typographic tools and skills, in order that these can be translated into modern practice.

Basically this book discusses three main issues: the design and layout of instructional materials, the language in which they are written, and how to evaluate the finished product. Each issue is important: by considering them in combination more effective text will be produced.

Acknowledgements

Many people have helped in the preparation of *Designing Instructional Text*, and although I can thank them here, it is impossible to name them all.

However, I can mention some. Peter Burnhill was responsible for the initial design of the first two editions of this text, and he has given me invaluable advice throughout. John Morin and John Coleman prepared much of the artwork. Doreen Waters helped Margaret Woodward to word-process the text. Helen Carley of Kogan Page urged me on. I am very grateful to these people and to the many others who have helped in one way or another with the production of this text.

James Hartley

1 Choosing a page-size

This chapter considers how choosing an appropriate page-size for a book or document determines subsequent decisions about the detailed planning of the work. Here I discuss the advantages and limitations of choosing a page-size from the range of standard sizes recommended by the International Organization for Standardization.

Printed materials come in many shapes and sizes. Until recently there have been no specific rules or guidelines which might suggest to writers, designers or printers why they should choose one page-size in preference to any other. The research literature on legibility and textbook design offers little help, for page-size is not an issue that features in many textbooks on typographic research. Why then do I choose to open my guide to designing instructional text by discussing page sizes?

Many people expect a review of typographic design to begin with issues such as type-sizes, type-faces and line-lengths. Indeed, the first question that an editor of a forthcoming journal once asked me was, 'What type-size should I use?' However, it is important to realize that the choice for this variable is already constrained by earlier decisions. Clearly we do not expect to find large type-sizes in a pocket dictionary nor a single column of print in a daily newspaper. These examples are extreme, but they illustrate the point. The choice of page-size comes first, and this affects the choices that are available for subsequent decisions.

The size of the page (and these days, the electronic screen) determines the size of the overall visual display. The reader needs to be able to scan and read this display easily, be it large like a wall chart, or small like a pocket timetable. The reader needs to be able to scan, read and focus on both the gross and the fine details. The size of the page or screen constrains the decisions that writers and designers make about these details.

The choice of an appropriate page-size is not always easy. A number of factors contribute to decisions about which page-size to use. Perhaps the most important one is some knowledge of how the information is going to be used. Other factors are reader preferences, the costs of production and marketing, basic paper sheet sizes and, more generally, the need to conserve resources and avoid waste.

Standard page-sizes

In the case of printed texts, one of the most obvious things that can be wasted is the paper itself. It is for this reason that there is great interest in manufacturing *standard* page-sizes, and the International Organization for Standardization has achieved an intriguing solution to this problem.

The page-sizes that we commonly see are cut from much larger basic sheets which have been folded several times. The present-day variety in page-sizes results from manufacturers using different sizes for their basic printing sheets and folding them in different ways. If the basic printing sheets were all one standard size, however, and the method of folding them allowed for little if any wastage at the cutting stage, then great economies could be achieved.

As an aside we may note that the need to rationalize paper sizes has been discussed for a long time in information printing. In 1798, for example, the French government prescribed a standard for official documents based on the proportion of 1:1.41 with a basic printing sheet of one square metre in area. In 1911, Wilhelm Oswald proposed 1:1.414 (that is, $1:\sqrt{2}$) as the 'world format'. In 1922 the German standard, DIN 476, was published. For this standard the ratio of $1:\sqrt{2}$ was retained with a basic printing sheet size of one square metre. The German standard, together with the A, B and C series of sizes, was adopted in 1958 by the International Organization for Standardization (ISO). Today the ISO series is recommended by the 50 or more national standards bodies which together make up the ISO.

The dimensions of the sizes in the ISO A and B series of sizes are set out below. The C series relates to envelope sizes for use with standard-sized documents and need not concern us here. In the United Kingdom the A series is now well known, especially the more commonly used A4 and A5 sizes. The B series, which is rooted in the same principle as the A series, and whose sizes fall in between those of the A series is, however, not so common.

ISO series of trimmed paper sizes:

A series		B series	
Designation	Size (mm)	Designation	Size (mm)
A0	841 x 1189	B0	1000 x 1414
A1	594 x 841	B1	707 x 1000
A2	420 x 594	B2	500 x 707
A3	297 x 420	B3	353 x 500
A4	210 x 297	B4	250 x 353
A5	148 x 210	B5	176 x 250
A6	105 x 148	B6	125 x 176
A7	74 x 105	B7	88 x 125
A8	52 x 74	B8	62 x 88
A9	37 x 52	B9	44 x 62
A10	26 x 37	B10	31 x 44

The unifying principle of the ISO-recommended range of sizes is that a rectangle with sides in the ratio of $1:\sqrt{2}$ can be halved or doubled to produce a series of rectangles *each of which will retain the proportions*

Figure 1/1

ISO paper sizes.

(1) This diagram illustrates the principle of construction and shows that the ratio of the sides of the rectangle is the same as that of the side of a square to its diagonal.

(2) This illustrates the fit between the A and the B series of sizes. For example, B5 falls between A5 and A4, and is geometrically similar.

(3) A rectangle of non-standard proportions. Note that the process of halving generates two geometrically dissimilar series of rectangles.

(4) A rectangle of standard proportions. This case is unique in that halving generates geometrically similar rectangles at each point in the series.

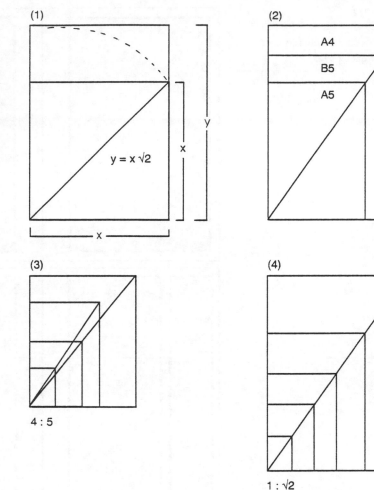

of the original (see Figure 1/1). A rectangle of any other proportion will generate geometrically similar rectangles only at every other point in the process of halving or doubling (Figure 1/1).

As the pages of a book are made by folding the larger basic printing sheet in half – once, twice, three times or more – all the pages made from a standard size basic sheet will be in the ratio of $1{:}\sqrt{2}$. Basic sheets which do not conform to this standard do not exhibit the property of geometric similarity when folded to form pages of a book, and this can create waste.

We may note at this point, of course, that documents can be bound at the top (notebook style) or on the left, and that they may be arranged in a vertical (portrait) or horizontal (landscape) style. These variations allow for a variety of page layouts (see Figure 1/2).

However, the astute reader will recognize that I have not chosen an ISO page-size for this book and will rightly ask, 'Why not?' The answer lies in the fact that, as noted earlier, a number of factors contribute to

Figure 1/2

Some possible subdivisions of
ISO standard pages.

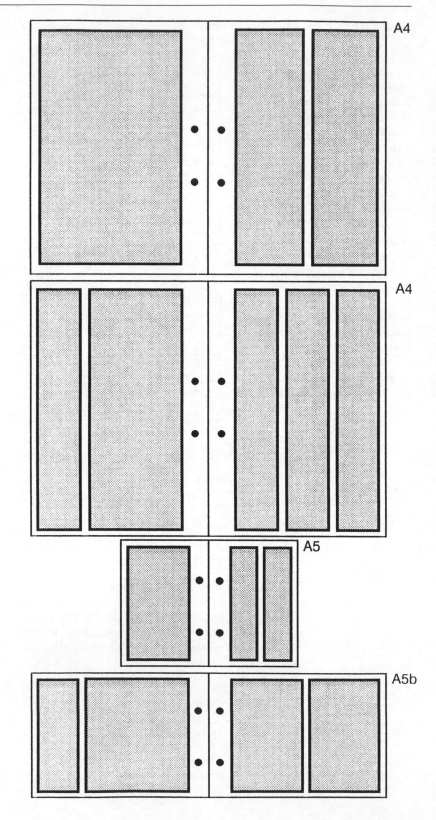

decisions about which page-size to use, and that some of these may seem more important than others.

Before planning can begin the designer/author has to ask a number of questions, such as:

1. How, when and where will this document be used?
2. How will the document be multiplied/printed/displayed?
3. Do additional specialists need to be consulted?
4. What costs and marketing factors are relevant, and will they influence the design decisions?

In considering question 1, the designer will take into account issues such as:

1a. The weight and size of the finished product and its orientation (horizontal, vertical, or square). Heavy books affect portability and handling.
1b. The method of binding to be used: binding affects ease of opening and thus ease of use.
1c. The storage system likely to be used (shelves, files, etc.): A4 books may be difficult to shelve.
1d. Type-sizes and type-styles.
    Is the work to be read at a hand-held reading distance, or some other?
    In good light?
    In association with other activities?
    By younger/older people, with good/poor sight?
    Will the work involve foreign language characters, mathematical characters, or special fonts?

In considering question 2 the designer will take into account issues such as:

2a. What constraints the method of reproduction will have on the design decisions.
2b. How the choice of page-size will affect these decisions.
2c. Whether the book will be printed in units of 2, 4, 8, 16 or 32-page sections and how this will affect page size.
2d. Is the work likely to be repeatedly copied, which will degrade its legibility?

In considering question 3 the designer will take into account issues such as:

3a. What role is to be played by the printer (if one is not using desk-top publishing systems oneself)? What printing machine is available? An injudiciously chosen page-size can mean that fewer pages can be printed at one time, and the image area of the printing machine to be used can have a big impact on the cost. If large numbers of copies are required then the increase in costs can be considerable.
3b. Do photographers, illustrators, etc. need to be consulted?

In considering question 4 the designer will take into account issues such as:

4a. What can readers/distributors afford?
4b. Do we need an 'advertising' style?
4c. Is paper quality important?
4d. Do we need a second colour?

All of these issues will be addressed in different places in this book. Here my concern is to indicate that many interrelated decisions need to be made and many of these, in fact, depend upon the choice of page-size.

In choosing the page-size for this third edition of *Designing Instructional Text* I have given more weight to the view that A4 is not a particularly useful size for hand-held reading. A4 is good for presenting notices and structured text which contains large illustrative materials.
One limitation, however, is that the double-page spread occupies a large space when an A4 book is open. A4 books are perhaps, therefore, more appropriate for using on large desks.

In addition, I have also given more weight to the notion that A4 books are more difficult to shelve and, my publisher assures me, to display in bookshops!

It is considerations such as these which come first when designing instructional text. After these decisions have been made (but not necessarily finalized) we can begin to think more about the details of typography. But even now, we still need to think in grosser terms – about how the text should be spaced – before turning to the finer details of type-sizes and type-faces.

▼

Summary

1. The choice of page-size comes first and determines subsequent typographic decisions.
2. The choice is mainly related to how the text is going to be used.
3. The ISO page-sizes have a number of virtues, but the practical limitations of some of the ISO page-sizes mean that other considerations must also be borne in mind when choosing the page-size.

Suggested further reading

Miles, J (1987) *Design for Desktop Publishing*, London: Gordon Fraser.
Misanchuk, E R (1992) *Preparing Instructional Text: Document design using desktop publishing*, Englewood Cliffs, NJ: Educational Technology Publications.

2 Basic planning decisions

This chapter discusses the importance of advance planning in the layout of instructional materials. Here I outline the rationale and use of the typographic reference grid and the value of a document specification chart or style sheet.

The advent of desk-top publishing systems provides the writer of instructional text with an opportunity not only to control the content of such texts, but also to determine the page-design of the work. What is not new is the *reader's* need to use the material without being confused by *ad hoc*, arbitrary and inconsistent arrangements of the text and its supporting devices (such as headings, tables, diagrams, graphs, lists, etc.).

To avoid such confusion requires now, as in the past, careful pre-planning of the work before it is committed to electronic storage and ultimately reproduction. The purpose then of these introductory chapters of this book is to outline basic practices and principles in typographic planning.

If we look at pages (or screens) of instructional text we can see that, unlike a novel, instructional text is complex. Instructional text usually contains a wide variety of components in addition to the text – such as listed information, numbered items, headings and sub-headings, diagrammatic presentations, tables, explanatory notes and pictorial features of many kinds. Typographically speaking, instructional materials are far more complex than novels. And again, typographically speaking, primary school texts are often more complex than those used in higher education.

Furthermore, much of this material is not read continuously. The learner's focus of attention often ranges from one place on the page (or screen) to somewhere else: to another page or screen, to the instructor, to the task in hand, to the blackboard, to another text, to other learners and, of course, back again to that same place on the page (or screen). The layout of the text must support this situation by providing a consistent frame of reference within which the learner can move about, leave and return without confusion.

The principal weakness of much instructional material is that it lacks consistency in the positioning of these functionally related parts. In primary school textbooks, for example, the relative position of the illustrations and of the text which refers to them frequently changes, both within a page and from page to page. So, as the book is being used, the learner must constantly be asking: 'Where am I supposed to go from here?' (Examples to illustrate this point are presented in Chapter 7.)

This kind of confusion in the sequential organization and the grouping of the parts shows not only a lack of rigour in the initial planning of the pages, but also a weakness in bridging the gap between typographical planning and print production. If one inspects many printed texts it is not hard to come to the conclusion that they are often composed page by page *during* production, on a sort of 'let's put this here' basis. Such a procedure produces inconsistency from page to page, particularly in terms of the spacing and the positioning of related components, such as headings and related paragraphs, illustrations and their captions, etc. One way to avoid this problem is to plan ahead, using a typographic grid.

The reference grid

In the days of hot-metal typesetting the typographic reference grid was an essential element for planning and communicating the design requirements to the printer. Today, it is still useful to consider what such grids achieve when planning one's own text. As can be seen from Figure 2/1a, a *basic reference grid* is a system of numbered coordinates which maps out the *information area* of the page in identically dimensioned modules of space. These modules are determined by making decisions about line length and inter-line space (see Chapter 3).

The information area is that part of the page outside which no printed matter will appear. For many books this information area is a clearly defined rectangle of print surrounded by the margins. In such cases the area devoted to the margins may occupy as much as 40–50 per cent of the page area. (This practice stems from the time when books were bought in sheet form to be folded, trimmed and specially bound in leather by the purchaser for inclusion in a private library. In the case of a book published in several sizes, the size of the information area remained constant. It was the width of the margins and the quality of the paper which helped to determine the size and price of the book: the wider the margins, the larger the book and the higher its price.)

The visual consequences of such past commercial and technical practices still tend to influence thinking about the aesthetics of page design. Nonetheless, today's designer of instructional text is usually more interested in using the space of the page in a manner which is dictated by the structure of the information than in forcing the print to fit rigidly into rectangular blocks.

Generally speaking, at the top, bottom and opening edge of the document, a margin of about 10 mm minimum is necessary for technical reasons associated with the print production process. The fourth margin (the inner or binding edge margin) is a special case. Here, thought should be given to factors which may indicate the need for a wider margin. For example, the printed page may be copied at some time and the copies punched for filing with other material. The binding system itself may involve the punching of pages, or it may be of the kind that causes some part of the edge of the page to be hidden from view. Indeed the binding system may be such that text or diagrams printed too close to the binding edge may curve inwards and be difficult to read. So, since text appears on both the front and the back of the page, a margin of about 25 mm is usually necessary at the binding edge of *both* left- and right-hand pages.

With these arrangements in mind we can now decide on the precise dimensions of the usable area of the page (the information area). The maximum permissible *depth* of the area will be specified in terms of the number of possible lines of text, including such lines as may be required for page numbers, running heads and other points of reference. As regards the maximum permissible *width* of the information area, a typographer's preference will be for measures which will subdivide readily to provide a series of column widths and inter-column spaces.

The basic grid is thus the foundation for drawing the *master reference grid* which is to be used in specifying the particular design requirements of the work in hand (see Figure 2/1b). To construct the master reference grid, decisions about the number of columns, the width of the columns, and the space between the columns will be made. Similarly, decisions need to be made about the number of lines per page, and the amount of space which is to be left before and after headings and between items of text. Furthermore, the position and the dimensions of the spaces allocated to the captions or diagrams and illustrations will be decided at this point (see Figures 2/1c and 2/1d). It is important to note, in order to avoid inconsistency, that the spaces between items are whole multiples of the line-feed dimension and are not changed from page to page.

In the past these grids were printed in pale blue, and galley proofs of the text were pasted on to them to ensure consistency throughout the document. If photo-composition was being used, the pale blue did not reproduce. Today, now that desk-top publishing systems are more easily available, designers may not wish or need to use a typographic reference grid. I have, however, described the grid above in order to make the general point that instructional text has to be planned carefully in advance of production.

The document specification or 'style sheet'

So far I have suggested that drawing up the typographic reference grid precedes drawing up what is termed the document specification or 'style sheet'. However, much of this decision making goes hand-in-hand. For both traditional and desk-top publishing the role of the document

Figure 2/1a

A basic reference grid.
The grid maps out the
information area of
the page. The
information (text,
illustrations, etc.)
need not fill this area,
but should not extend
beyond it.

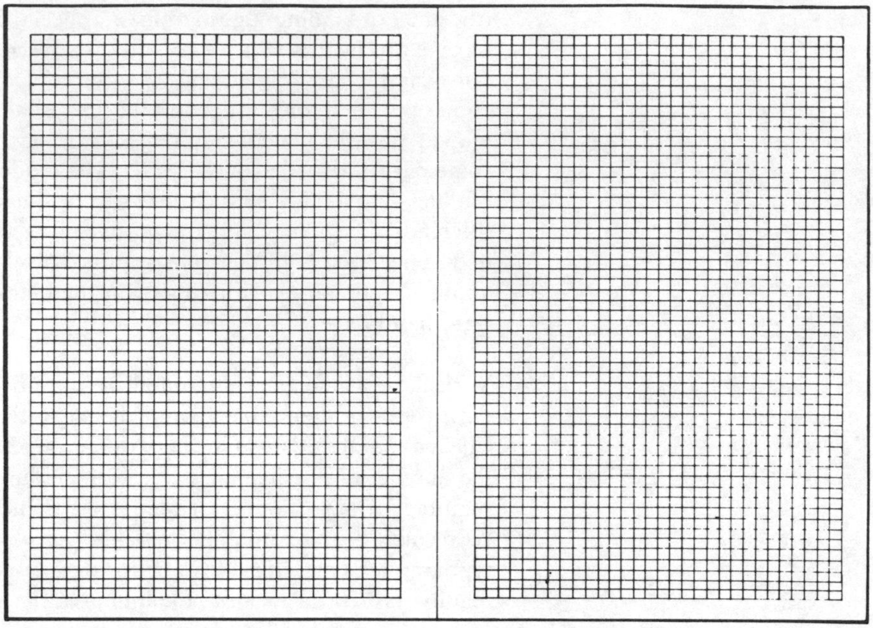

Figure 2/1b

A master reference
grid for a particular
document. This grid
specifies the particular
dimensional
requirements of the
work.

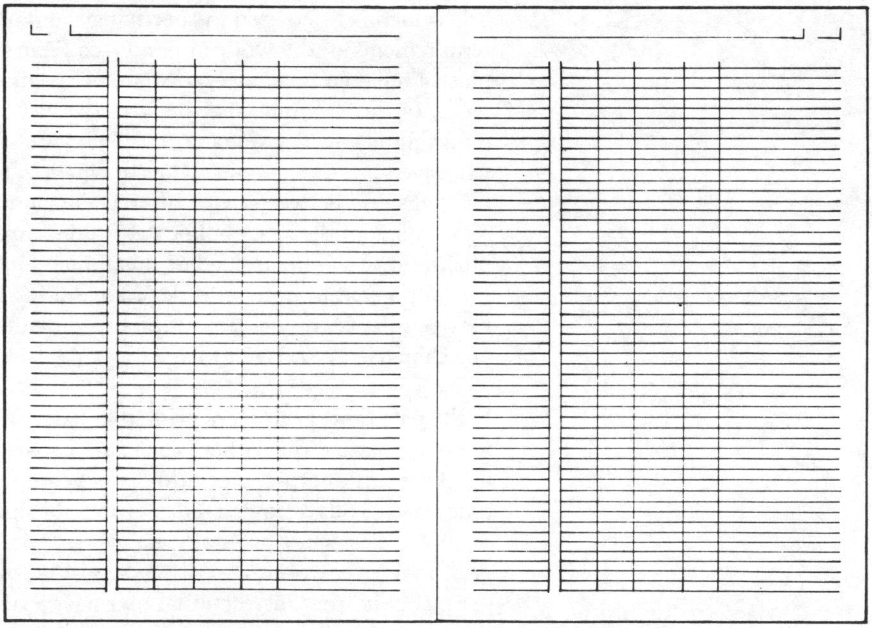

Figure 2/1c

How the grid and the text relate. Note the widest margin is in the 'gutter'. Also note that the side headings fall within the information area, and not in the margins as such.

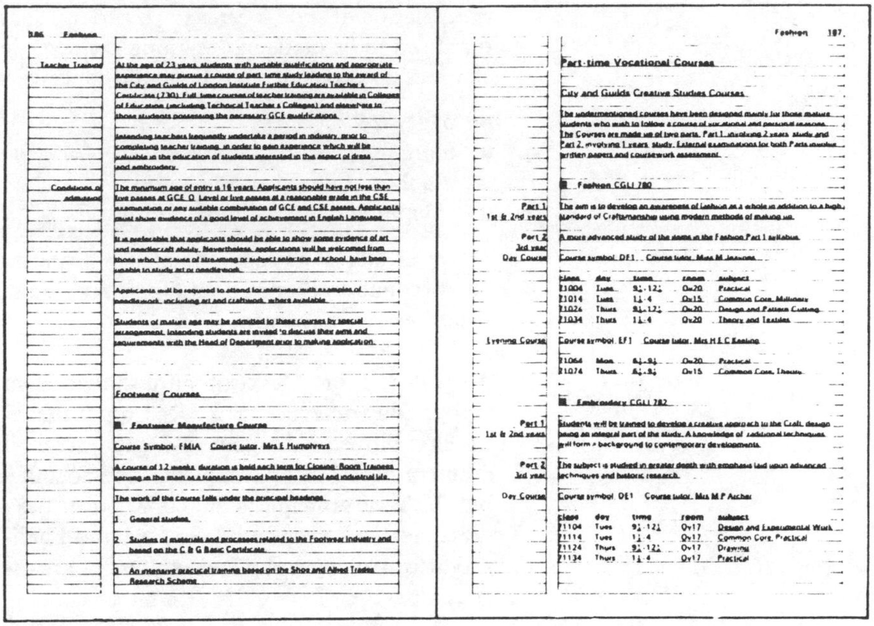

Figure 2/1d

The final printed page. The grid lies 'invisibly' behind the printed image and so provides a consistent and reliable frame of reference for the reader throughout the work.

Spaces between items are whole multiples of the line-feed dimension, and this is consistent throughout the text.
Horizontal shifts are similarly predetermined for the whole of the text.

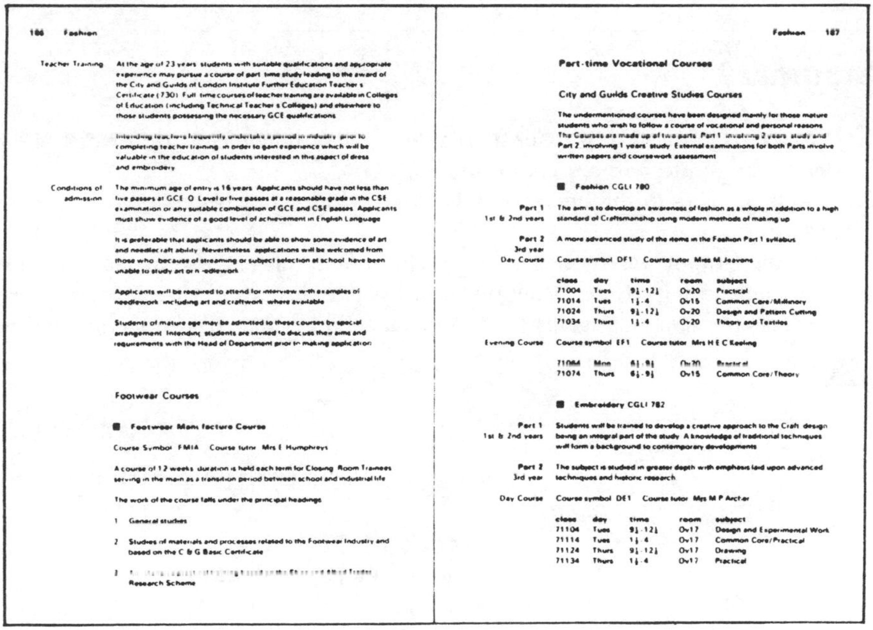

specification or style sheet is to record in advance all the major decisions that need to be made in designing the text. So far, in terms of this chapter, decisions need to be made concerning the

- page size
- margins
- number of lines per page, and
- column and intercolumn widths.

However, decisions concerning such a specification also need to take into account decisions about type-sizes and type-faces, and it is to these issues that we now turn.

A style sheet for a desk-top publishing system is not as rigid as was the typographic reference grid. Desk-top publishing and word-processing systems allow the designer to explore freely the effects of making different decisions on samples of the document before finalizing them. But the basic principle is the same. To ensure consistency for the reader, these decisions need to be assessed and finalized in advance of the production of the complete text, and not made from page to page as one goes along.

Summary

1. Printed pages need to provide a reliable frame of reference within which the reader can move about, leave and return without confusion.
2. Planning pages to this end should be done before work begins on setting the text and designing the artwork.
3. The typographic reference grid is a useful tool in this respect for planning instructional materials.
4. Although such grids are being replaced by style sheets and specification charts, the basic principle remains the same: decisions need to be made in advance of production and not from page to page.

Suggested further reading

Goldring, M (1984) 'Has the revolution in the composition of type improved typography?', *Information Design Journal*, 4, 1, 77–82.

Goldring, M and Hackelsberger, A (1973) 'A standard specification for print production', *The Penrose Annual*, 66.

Miles, J (1987) *Design for Desktop Publishing*, London: Gordon Fraser.

3 Type-sizes and inter-line spacing

This chapter discusses factors affecting the choice of type-sizes and inter-line spacing. Here I avoid giving advice on choosing a particular type-size in favour of pointing out general principles that underlie decision making at this point.

In Chapters 1 and 2 I have explained how major decisions, such as the choice of page-size and the overall arrangement of the information on the page, help to determine the choice of type-sizes and inter-line spacing.

As we move on to consider these more detailed decisions we find more research on the topic. Several researchers have made suggestions concerning the appropriate size of type for reading matter and have given advice on related factors such as line-length and line-spacing. Tinker (1963) and Watts and Nisbet (1974) provide good summaries of this literature.

Unfortunately, much of the research in these areas is not very helpful to designers of instructional materials. This is principally because variables such as type-size, line-length and inter-line space have not been studied in the 'real-life' context of instructional text. Most researchers, for example, have considered issues of type-size in short, simple settings of continuous prose. Furthermore, they have usually used 'justified' text – that is, text which (*unlike* this text) has a straight left- and right-hand edge and which is achieved by inconsistent word spacing from line to line.

Type-sizes

As noted earlier, it is conventional to begin texts of this kind with a discussion of type-sizes. Here I shall only note one or two points of detail concerning size *per se* before pointing to other issues.

There are many different measurement systems used in the printing industry but, with the advent of desk-top publishing, these may get reduced. Some measures still remain, however. The most basic one for measuring type-size is that of the 'point'. (A point measures 0.0138 inches.) Typical type-sizes in textbooks are 10, 11 and 12 point. The 'small print' (in legal documents, for example) may be 6 or 8 point, and this is too small for most people to read with ease. Larger sizes (such as

Figure 3/1

Some examples of type-sizes

This type-size is 8 point

This type-size is 10 point

This type-size is 12 point

This type-size is 14 point

This type-size is 16 point

14, 18 and 24 point) are used for headings and display purposes (see Figure 3/1). In this text the typographic setting of the text is $9^1/_2$ point on $11^1/_2$ point. This indicates that there is an extra space of 2 points between the lines of print. The main text headings are set in 14 point bold, and the chapter headings in 28 point bold.

A confusing aspect of past research in this field has been the tendency to recommend the use of specific type-sizes without proper regard for the fact that the specified size of a type-face (say 12 point) does *not* refer to the dimensions of the image of the printed characters as seen by the reader. The specified size refers instead to the depth of space that was required by the line of metal type when it was set with the minimum line-to-line space. The actual image size could vary within this space.

Figure 3/2, for instance, shows the same sentence printed in one size of type but in five different type-faces. As can be seen, at best, type-size is but a first approximation to image size. And, as the figure shows, the choice of type-face is important in determining the perceived size.

Figure 3/2

The same designated type-size produces different sized images with different type-faces.

This is 12 point Times Roman

This is 12 point Palatino

This is 12 point Helvetica

This is 12 point Century Schoolbook

This is 12 point Bookman

So it is not my intention here to recommend specific type-sizes for use in printing instructional materials, especially as the specified size of a set of characters can only be a rough approximation to the actual size of the printed image of the letters and the words. However, I would like to outline one approach to the problem of choosing a type-size for a text. At root, this concerns two factors:

1. Designers need to choose a maximum permissible line-length which, when related to the type-size, will not obstruct the proper and sensible phrasing of the information; and
2. designers need to consider the relationship between the word-spacing and the line-spacing of the information.

Line-length and type-sizes

Designers need to examine their text carefully to look for problems which could arise if they choose too large a type-face. For example, in books for small children the maximum permissible length of a line is often limited by the type-size to being three or four words long. In this case the syntactic grouping of the words in the lines is difficult to achieve. Thus one of the primary dimensions to be considered when thinking about type-sizes is the *width* of the character groups and syntactically structured word-strings, and not the vertical dimension of the characters *per se*. This is shown in Figure 3/3.

Figure 3/3

How increases in type-size affect the length of a phrase as well as the depth.

Once upon a time

Once upon a time

Once upon a time

Once upon a time

Word-spacing

In many texts the lines are set 'justified'. As noted above, with justified text all of the lines are of equal length, and they are made so by varying the spacing between the words on each line and by hyphenating or breaking words at the line ends. However, in 'unjustified' text, the word-spacing is consistent throughout the text, and the line endings are more ragged (as here). I want to argue that, for instructional text, word groups need to be allowed to vary in length as the sense demands. Furthermore, when the word-spacing is of a fixed amount throughout the work (as in this text) no words need to be broken at line ends.

Figure 3/4

The width of the spaces between the words is normally that of a lower-case 'i'.

Once█upon█a█time

Onceiuponiaitime

Once upon a time

Word-spacing should be large enough to allow the grouping of characters – the word-images – to be differentiated clearly. Typographers suggest that this is achieved when the width of the word-space is about 25 per cent of the designated type-size. This, traditionally, is the width of the space allowed for the lower-case letter 'i' (see Figure 3/4).

Line-spacing

The line-space refers to the distance from the base-line of one line of text to the base-line of the next line (see Figure 3/5). The line-space is minimal when it is the same dimension as the type-size. In this minimal state, the interlinear space (the *apparent* space between the lines of words) may appear to be less than the space between the words.

Figure 3/5

The relationships between type-size and line-spacing.

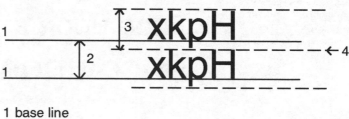

1 base line
2 line-space
3 type-size
4 interline space
  (in this case, zero; ie type-size = line-space).

To make text easier to read it is conventional to open out the lines to create a clear difference between the inter-linear gap and the word-spacing. This procedure reduces the danger of optical bridging between the lines. Typographic practice suggests that satisfactory spacing is achieved when the minimum line-space dimension is increased by an amount equivalent to the dimension specified for the word-spacing of the text (see Figure 3/6).

So, if the word-spacing is specified as 25 per cent of the type-size, then the line-space should be not less than 125 per cent of the type-size. For example, with a type-size that occupies no more than 4 mm in the overall depth of the character image, the word-spacing would be 1 mm and the line-space (ie base-line to base-line) 5 mm.

Implications for the style sheet

In the past, when metal type was set by hand, the line-spacing would be inserted as the lines were set. Today, when information is assembled electronically or through a keyboard system of one kind or another, line-spacing is included at the same time as the text is keyed.

Figure 3/6

The relationship between word-spacing and line-spacing.

In the top figure the type is 'set solid', i.e. there is no extra line-spacing.

In the bottom figure the type is set with extra line-spacing that is the same dimension as the word-spacing.

Once upon a time
there was a piece
of wood. It was not

Once upon a time there was a piece of wood.
It was not the best wood, but just a common piece,
such as we use in stoves and fireplaces to kindle
a fire and warm our homes in winter. I can't say
how it happened, but the fact is that one fine day
this piece of wood happened to be in the shop of an

Once upon a time
there was a piece
of wood. It was not

Once upon a time there was a piece of wood.
It was not the best wood, but just a common piece,
such as we use in stoves and fireplaces to kindle
a fire and warm our homes in winter. I can't say
how it happened, but the fact is that one fine day
this piece of wood happened to be in the shop of an

Decisions concerning type-sizes and line-space therefore have to be made in advance and entered on to the specification chart or style sheet.

In terms of this chapter, decisions have to be made concerning:

● type-faces (see next chapter)
● type-sizes
    chapter title
    running head
    introductory summary
    body of text
    headings
    examples
    captions
    references
    indexes

- inter-line feed
  below chapter title
  below running head
  below introductory summary
  body of text
  between paragraphs
  above main headings
  below main headings
  above secondary headings
  below secondary headings
  above tertiary headings
  above tables and figures
  below tables and figures
  above captions
  below captions
  above end summary

Again it may be profitable to explore the effects of manipulating these factors with samples of text before finalizing these decisions.

Summary

1. The advice given by typographic researchers on optional type-sizes for specific purposes needs to be considered with caution.
2. The main dimension to be considered in choosing the type-size is the line-length.
3. Optimum line-spacing is achieved when the minimum line-to-line dimension is increased by an amount equivalent to the dimension specified for the word-spacing of the text.
4. Details concerning the type-faces, type-sizes and the inter-line spacing required both for the body of the text and for its special requirements (eg, headings, captions) need to be decided in advance and entered on to the style sheet.

References

Tinker, M A (1963) *Legibility of Print*, Ames: Iowa State University Press.
Watts, L and Nisbet, J (1974) *Legibility in Children's Books*, London: National Foundation for Educational Research.

Suggested further reading

Black, A (1990) *Typefaces for Desktop Publishing: A user guide*, London: Architecture Design & Technology Press.

4 Choosing type-faces

This chapter discusses factors affecting the choice of type-faces. Here I point out that such choices are affected by practical matters: what is the purpose of the text, what is available and what should be avoided.

One particular source of confusion to novice designers is how to choose an appropriate type-face from the bewildering range currently available. For example, one encyclopaedia of type-faces published in 1930 listed over 2,350 entries, and it is estimated that by now there are well over 10,000 type-faces available. Furthermore, many desk-top systems offer their users a huge variety of choice – so how should we decide which to use?

One way of classifying type-faces (or fonts as they are often loosely called in desk-top publishing systems) is in terms of those that have *serifs* (finishing strokes at the ends of letters) and those that do not (*sans-serif*). This paragraph is printed in Times New Roman, a face with serifs. The following paragraph is printed in Helvetica, a sans-serif face, to illustrate the effects.

Another question I am commonly asked (almost as frequently as 'What type-size should I use?') is, 'Should I use a serif or a sans-serif type-face?' It seems to me that the available research really gives no clear guidance on this issue, so one has to make a decision based upon good practice and common sense.

Some people recommend that faces with serifs be used for the body of the text and that faces without serifs be used for headings, or for other purposes (such as to differentiate examples from the body of the text). Others consider that sans-serif type-faces are more legible in the smaller sizes (eg, 6 and 8 point) and go on to argue that sans-serif type-faces are better for text that is not intended for continuous reading (eg, reference works, tables, catalogues, etc.). The Royal National Institute for the Blind recommends the use of sans-serif type-faces for small blocks of instructional text for visually impaired readers. (See Chapter 11.)

Capital letters

Words printed in capital letters contain less distinctive information per unit of space than do words set in lower-case characters of the same type-size, so this makes groups of them more difficult to read.

IT IS GENERALLY BELIEVED THAT WHOLE PARAGRAPHS OF TEXT SET IN CAPITAL LETTERS ARE MORE DIFFICULT TO READ THAN ARE PARAGRAPHS SET IN NORMAL UPPER- AND LOWER-CASE LETTERS. THE USE OF STRINGS OF WORDS IN CAPITALS FOR MAIN HEADINGS (OR SMALL CAPITALS FOR SECONDARY HEADINGS) MAY BE SATISFACTORY BECAUSE, NORMALLY, SUCH HEADINGS ARE SURROUNDED BY SPACE WHICH AIDS THEIR PERCEPTION. ON THE WHOLE, THOUGH, THE USE OF CAPITAL LETTERS SHOULD BE KEPT TO A MINIMUM. APART FROM SPECIALIZED USE IN MATHEMATICAL WORK, CAPITAL LETTERS ARE BEST RESERVED FOR THE FIRST LETTER OF A SENTENCE (INCLUDING HEADINGS), AND FOR THE FIRST LETTER OF PROPER NOUNS.

Writers occasionally capitalize words as a means of emphasis. This is understandable when handwriting or typewriting offers no other method for doing this, apart from underlining. However, this change in the appearance of the word-image may confuse the less-able reader. Underlining, on the other hand, may cause technical problems. If a change from the norm is really necessary, then the **bold version** of the lower-case letters can provide it without radically changing the geometrical characteristics of the word-image.

Ellington and Race (1993) provide some interesting illustrations of the effects of different type-faces when they are used in slides and other projected materials. Of particular relevance here is the reduced legibility of such projected text when it is printed in capital letters.

Italicized letters

Sloping or 'italic' characters were introduced originally into printed books in the sixteenth century as a means of setting more characters to the line, the style of letters being more compressed than the vertically drawn and rounded forms of the normal lower-case character set. Again, it is commonly believed that continuous italic text is harder to read than the more conventional typographic settings.

Today, italicized characters are often used in instructional materials as a means of emphasizing a word in the text, for the titles of books when these appear in the writing of the text, in bibliographic references, and sometimes for abstracts in journal articles.

Numerals

The arabic numerals associated with some type-faces assume an up-and-down appearance when set in groups. Numerals of this kind are called non-ranging or 'old style' (see Figure 4/1). For instructional materials, standard or ranging numerals are to be preferred to the non-ranging kind. In mathematical text, numerals which align with one another, both vertically and horizontally, are obviously necessary. Non-ranging numerals may confuse the young reader.

Figure 4/1

Left: Ranging numerals.
Right: Non-ranging numerals.

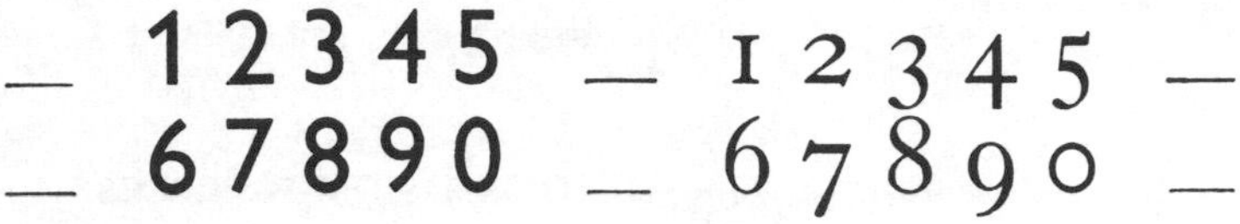

1 2 3 4 5   1 2 3 4 5
6 7 8 9 0   6 7 8 9 0

Mathematical textbooks and worksheets provide particularly difficult design problems, and require careful specification in advance if spatial consistency is to be maintained throughout the text. It is now becoming the practice for authors to write mathematical text on appropriate grid sheets.

It must be remembered, of course, that young readers cannot be expected to know automatically why a change from the norm has taken place. This particularly applies to the printing of individual words in bold or in colour. Young readers need to be taught these conventions. (Box 4/1 shows how even the smallest of typographic conventions has to be learned.)

Box 4.1   Shows how even the smallest of typographic conventions has to be learned.

Ann Henshaw asked some 5-year-old children to explain to her why we had periods or 'dots' at the end of sentences. A sample of the replies is as follows:

'Well ... the ones with dots on should have dots on. Its the words.... Well sometimes you don't need one. When you've had enough of doing dots you don't do one 'cos then it won't make your arm ache.'

'Some words need them. Some words don't.'

'It's for if you go off the page and go to the desk ... you stop ... you don't start again ... you start again after a minute or two.'

'It's to tell you when they've finished.'

'When they have to finish a page of writing they have them ... if there's no room and you have to go on to another page they put a fullstop (period) there.

'It stops you from doing writing.'

'It's at the end of your work you put one. You get told off if you don't.'

'It's to finish a sentence. If you don't put a fullstop and you write a letter people might think you've forgotten to post the other half.'

'Look,' (reading 'It is another day', 'Then it is the fullstop.') 'See? ... I miss out a bit of my voice and then I start again.'

Extracts reproduced courtesy of Ann Henshaw.

Finally, we need to remember that the use of devices such as capital letters, colour, underlining, italic and bold need to be used sparingly as they can lose their significance when they are used in combination or to excess. Misanchuk (1992) comments that,

There is widespread agreement that the number of fonts used should be strictly limited. . . . An often repeated rule of thumb is to limit font choices to two – one serifed for body type, and one sans-serif for headings and/or figure labels and captions – and to use different sizes and styles (italic, bold) to indicate levels of heading.

Choosing type-faces

In practice, choosing a type-face really means:

1. Considering the purpose of the text.
2. Making sure that the chosen sizes and weights required for the work are available.
3. Making sure that the character set contains not only the commonly used signs but also any special characters called for by the author's text.
4. Considering how well particular type-faces will withstand repeated copying.

Certain type-faces seem more appropriate in some situations than others. Neither Gothic, for example, nor Balloon is very helpful for instructional text. Some type-faces appear to have emotional connotations for some readers and readers have many preferences. Regrettably, however, research has failed so far to be able to produce any clearcut findings in this respect that might suggest which type-face is appropriate for which context.

However, when printing instructional materials, it seems that there are two kinds of type-faces to avoid (Black, 1990). These are:

1. Those which may confuse the learner by exhibiting idiosyncratic features in the shape of particular characters or in the overall design of the character set; and
2. Those which may readily suffer loss of identity when printing or copying is less than perfect. Factors to be wary of in this latter connection are:
   - fine lines which may break down;
   - small internal spaces which may fill in;
   - strong contrast between thick and thin strokes which may cause a dazzle effect, especially when the print is on very white or glossy paper; and
   - letters which appear to touch one another.

In general, instructional materials should be printed in characters which are firm in line, open and even in spacing and without any idiosyncratic features in their design. Such features should probably take priority over aesthetic considerations as the research suggests that what is aesthetically pleasing to some may not be so to others.

Style sheet implications

In terms of this chapter, decisions have to be made concerning the choice of type-faces for:

- the chapter title,
- the running heads,
- the introductory summary,
- the body of the text,
- the main, secondary and tertiary headings,
- the figure and table captions, and
- the text of these figures and tables where they are printed as part of the text (and not reproduced from other materials).

Summary

1. Serif and sans-serif type-faces have advantages and limitations. Care should be taken in deciding what is appropriate for the text in hand.
2. Capitals, italics, underlining, etc. should be used sparingly. Children need to be told what such changes are intended to indicate.
3. The choice of type-face is determined by practical matters – the nature of the text, what is available and what should be avoided.
4. Type-faces to avoid are those with idiosyncratic designs and those which will not withstand degradation when repeatedly copied.
5. The use of standard (ranging) numerals is to be preferred in mathematical materials, which should be planned on appropriate grid sheets.

References

Black, A (1990) *Typefaces for Desktop Publishing: A user guide*, London: Architecture Design & Technology Press.

Ellington, H and Race, P (1993) *Producing Teaching Materials* (2nd edn), London: Kogan Page.

Misanchuk, E R (1992) *Preparing Instructional Text: Document design using desktop publishing*, Englewood Cliffs, NJ: Educational Technology Publications.

Suggested further reading

Lewis, C and Walker, P (1989) 'Typographic influences on reading', *British Journal of Psychology*, 80, 2, 241–58.

5   Space and structure

In this chapter I discuss further how one can manipulate the vertical and the horizontal dimensions of a piece of text in order to clarify its underlying structure. The chapter concludes with a specification for the setting of this book.

One of my main arguments in this textbook is that how the designer uses the space on the page (or screen) greatly affects how easily the reader can understand and retrieve information from the text. Although the text is important – one cannot do without it – I want to argue that the clarity of the text can be enhanced by a rational and consistent use of the 'white space'.

Space plays an important role in clarifying text. It is space that separates letters from each other. It is space that separates words from each other. It is space (with punctuation) that separates phrases, clauses and paragraphs from each other; and it is space (with headings and subheadings) that separates subsections and chapters from one another.

There is some evidence, admittedly equivocal, from eye-movement research which suggests that these spatial cues are important aids to understanding text. It is argued, for instance, that with increasing maturity and experience, readers come to rely more heavily on such spatial cues to enhance their reading and search efficiency. It has been shown that the beginning of a line (and not its end) has a marked effect on eye-movement fixations, and that text which starts in an irregular manner (such as poetry or right-justified text) produces more regressive fixations (look backs) than does regularly spaced text.

In this book I maintain that consistent spacing:

1. Helps readers to see redundancies in the text and thus to read faster;
2. Helps readers to see more easily which bits of the text are personally relevant for them; and,
3. Helps readers to see the structure of the document as a whole.

Thus it helps them to understand its organization.

Vertical spacing

The spacing of a page can be considered from both a vertical and a horizontal point of view. Let us take vertical spacing first. The argument here is that the underlying structure of complex text can be demonstrated more clearly to the reader by a consistent and planned use of vertical spacing. In effect units of line-feed (vertical space) can be used consistently to separate out components of the text such as sentences, paragraphs, sub and major headings.

One simple way of using line-feed in this way is to use it in a proportional system. One can, for example, start each sentence on a new line within a paragraph (no extra line-feed); separate paragraphs by one extra line-feed unit; separate subheadings from paragraphs by two extra lines above and one below them; and separate main headings from text by four extra lines above and two below them. In essence, this is the system used in this book, except that I have not started new sentences on a new line within paragraphs. (That is a procedure that I reserve for more complex text.)

What is the effect of such an approach? Figure 5/1a shows a traditionally spaced piece of text, and Figure 5/1b shows a revised version using the system described above.

Such proportional systems are effective ways of ensuring consistent vertical spacing between the component parts of a piece of text.

Figure 5/1a

A traditionally spaced piece of text.

General

This section describes the care, maintenance and inspection of insulating rubber blankets. This section is re-issued to delete reference to the KS-13602 cleaner; this has been superseded by the B cleaning fluid (AT-8236).

Description

An insulating rubber blanket is made of flat, flexible sheets of black rubber. These sheets do not contain either beaded edges or eyelets. The blankets are approximately 36 inches square, 1/10th inch thick and weigh approximately 7lbs. The electrical, weather and chemical resistance properties of the blanket are very good.
   Rubber-stamped on each blanket is a 'Return for Test' date. Blankets must be returned for testing by that date to the Western Electric Company – or other authorized agent. The blankets should be returned in rolls (3.1/2 ins. diameter) and wrapped properly so as to avoid damage. A replacement blanket will be made available when a blanket is returned for testing.

Inspection

Before using a blanket inspect it each time for cracks, cuts, tears or other mechanical damage as follows: . . .

Figure 5/1b

A revised version of Figure 5/1a.

General

This section describes the care, maintenance and
inspection of insulating rubber blankets.
This section is re-issued to delete reference to
the KS-13602 cleaner; this has been superseded by
the B cleaning fluid (AT-8236).

Description

An insulating rubber blanket is made of flat,
flexible sheets of black rubber.
These sheets do not contain either beaded edges
or eyelets.
The blankets are approximately 36 inches square,
1/10th inch thick and weigh approximately 7lbs.
The electrical, weather and chemical resistance
properties of the blanket are very good.
Rubber-stamped on each blanket is a 'Return for
Test' date.
Blankets must be returned for testing by that
date to the Western Electric Company – or other
authorized agent.
The blankets should be returned in rolls
(3.1/2 ins. diameter) and wrapped properly so
as to avoid damage.
A replacement blanket will be made available when
a blanket is returned for testing.

Inspection

Before using a blanket inspect it each time for
cracks, cuts, tears or other mechanical damage
as follows: . . .

Other systems (not proportional, but equally consistent) can be used
and, indeed, for more complex text one might wish to introduce
indentations in the text to convey further substructure.

Floating baseline

In this section on vertical spacing we should note that, if the vertical
spacing between the components of the text is to be consistent
throughout the text, then this leads to the idea that the text will have
what is called a *floating baseline*. This means that, in contrast to
traditional printing practice, the text does not stop at the same point on
every page, irrespective of its content. The stopping point on each page is
determined by the content rather than by the need to fill the page.

So, in terms of our style sheet or page layout specification, we can say the
text should have a specified number of lines plus or minus two.

This flexibility allows us to avoid 'widows' and 'orphans' – where a page might start with the last (half) line of a previous paragraph, or end with a heading, or the first line of a new paragraph.

Designing Instructional Text has such a floating baseline. The page layout allows for 51 lines of text plus or minus two. This means that one can use one extra line (or two) if a sentence or paragraph ends on the 51st line. It also means that headings do not appear as the last item on a page, nor do paragraphs end on the top line of the next page.
And, unlike traditional printing practice, the internal spacing of the text is not squeezed or expanded in order to make the text fit into a prescibed rectangle.

However, to conclude this section on a point of detail, one difficulty with this setting arises when the last line of the page falls in the middle of a paragraph, but it ends with a full stop. If we are using a line-space to denote the start of a new paragraph, then readers will not know when they turn over whether or not they are continuing with the previous paragraph, or starting a new one. With a floating baseline, however, we can continue and add the next line of the text at the bottom of the page, or we can carry over the original line to start the next page.

Horizontal spacing

One can consider the horizontal spacing of text in much the same way as we have considered the vertical spacing. That is to say we can look to see how we can use the horizontal spacing to separate and to group components of the text, and how we can vary the stopping point of horizontal text in accord with its content, rather than using arbitrary rules about line-lengths.

In traditional printing practice it is conventional for the columns of print to have a straight right- and left-hand edge. As we noted in Chapter 3, technically this is called *justified* composition. Justification is achieved by varying the spaces between the words and sometimes by using hyphenation. Indeed, in some cases with very narrow columns (eg, in newspaper composition or advertising copy), the spaces between the letters forming the words are also varied in order to force the text to fit a given length of line.

A different approach to setting text is to provide a consistent space between each word. Such a procedure produces *unjustified* composition – as in this book. Here there is the same amount of space between each word, and there are no word-breaks (or hyphenation): consequently the text has a ragged right-hand edge.

Experiments have shown that, despite much argument (see Misanchuk, 1992) there is little to choose between justified and unjustified text in terms of legibility, reading speed or comprehension. There are some indications, however, that unjustified composition might be more helpful for less-able readers (be they younger children or older adults).

Figure 5/2a

An example of justified text.

Now the sons of Jacob were twelve. The sons of
Leah: Reuben, Jacob's firstborn, and Simeon,
and Levi, and Judah, and Issachar, and Zebulun. The sons of Rachel: Joseph, and Benjamin.
And the sons of Bilhah, Rachel's handmaid:
Dan, and Naphtali. And the sons of Zilpah,
Leah's handmaid: Gad, and Asher. These are the
sons of Jacob, which were born to him in Padan-
aram.

Figure 5/2b

The same text set unjustified,
with consistent word-spacing.

Now the sons of Jacob were twelve. The sons of
Leah: Reuben, Jacob's firstborn, and Simeon,
and Levi, and Judah, and Issachar, and
Zebulun. The sons of Rachel: Joseph, and
Benjamin. And the sons of Bilhah, Rachel's
handmaid: Dan, and Naphtali. And the sons of
Zilpah, Leah's handmaid: Gad, and Asher.
These are the sons of Jacob, which were born to
him in Padan-aram.

Figure 5/2c

The same text with line-endings
determined by syntactic
considerations.

Now the sons of Jacob were twelve.
The sons of Leah:
Reuben, Jacob's firstborn,
and Simeon, and Levi, and Judah,
and Issachar, and Zebulun.
The sons of Rachel:
Joseph, and Benjamin.
And the sons of Bilhah, Rachel's handmaid:
Dan, and Naphtali.
And the sons of Zilpah, Leah's handmaid:
Gad, and Asher.
These are the sons of Jacob, which were born
to him in Padan-aram.

Figure 5/2d

The same text with line-
beginnings and line-endings
chosen to show the underlying
structure of the text.

Now the sons of Jacob were twelve.
The sons of Leah:
    Reuben, Jacob's firstborn,
    and Simeon, and Levi, and Judah,
    and Issachar, and Zebulun.
The sons of Rachel:
    Joseph, and Benjamin.
And the sons of Bilhar, Rachel's handmaid:
    Dan, and Naphtali.
And the sons of Zilpah, Leah's handmaid:
    Gad, and Asher.
These are the sons of Jacob, which were born
to him in Padan-aram.

Figure 5/2e

Additional spacing clarifies even
further the underlying structure
of the text.

```
Now the sons of Jacob were twelve.

    The sons of Leah:
        Reuben, Jacob's firstborn,
        and Simeon, and Levi, and Judah,
        and Issachar, and Zebulun.

    The sons of Rachel:
        Joseph, and Benjamin.

    And the sons of Bilhar, Rachel's handmaid:
        Dan, and Naphtali.

    And the sons of Zilpah, Leah's handmaid:
        Gad, and Asher.

These are the sons of Jacob, which were born
to him in Padan-aram.
```

None the less, it is doubtful whether these experimental studies have considered fully all of the advantages of unjustified text. One clear advantage is that one does not have to fill up each line with text: one can consider (as with vertical spacing) where best to end each line.

Figure 5/2a shows a piece of justified text. Figure 5/2b shows the same text set unjustified. Figure 5/2c shows what happens when syntactic groupings are considered. With unjustified text, for instance, it is possible to specify that no line should end with the first word of a new sentence, or that if the next-to-last word on a line is followed by a punctuation mark then this last word should be carried over to the next line.

Figure 5/2c is in fact based on Bradbury Thompson's design for *The Washburn College Bible* (see Thompson, 1988). This Bible is printed throughout in unjustified text, and line-endings are determined by syntactic groupings. *The Washburn College Bible* is actually a *lectern* bible. It is printed in large type to allow the minister to read it out loud to the congregation, and undoubtedly its typographical format helps the minister in this respect.

Figures 5/2d and 5/2e are additional suggestions which show how one can consider the *starting* as well as the *stopping* points in setting text of this kind. Here space and indentation are used to convey further the substructure.

Combining vertical and horizontal spacing

So far I have discussed vertical and horizontal spacing as though they were separate issues – which, of course, they are not. In all texts interrelated decisions need to be taken which depend upon the nature of the text. If the text consists of nothing but continuous prose, then (on an

A5 page) a single-column structure with normal paragraph indentation may be perfectly acceptable. If, however, the text consists of numerous small elements, all of which start on a new line, then using traditional indentation to denote new paragraphs can be misleading (see Figure 5/3). It is for reasons such as these that I generally advocate the use of line-spacing rather than indentation to denote the start of new paragraphs in instructional text.

Figure 5/3

Traditional indentation for the start of a new paragraph may distract the reader when the paragraphs are short.

The young of most mammals are born alive, instead of being hatched from eggs.

The young of all mammals are fed with their mother's milk.

All mammals have some hair or fur on their bodies.

All mammals have warm blood.

Figure 5/4a

A traditional setting for a piece of text containing a list.

The results of this investigation suggest that older students usually perform as well as or sometimes better than traditional entry ones, that the results are sometimes affected by the nature of the discipline, with mature students generally doing better in the Arts and Social Sciences than in the Sciences, and that there are sometimes sex differences in the results which are not wholly consistent: often mature women seem to do better than mature men but this is not always the case.

Figure 5/4b

A revised setting for the same text

The results of this investigation suggest that:

● older students usually perform as well as or sometimes better than traditional entry ones;

● the results are sometimes affected by the nature of the discipline, with mature students generally doing better in the Arts and Social Sciences than in the Sciences; and

● there are sometimes sex differences in the results which are not wholly consistent: often mature women seem to do better than mature men but this is not always the case.

Finally in this chapter we might note that the research has shown that readers usually prefer text to be set in a more open manner: thus readers generally prefer text set in the style of Figure 5/1b to that of Figure 5/1a. Furthermore, research has also shown that readers often recall more from text shown in the manner of Figure 5/2d than they do from text shown in the manner of Figure 5/2a. And, curiously enough, when asked to write out their recalls of texts set in different formats, readers write them out in the formats they are presented with (Hartley, 1993).

Readers also like lists of information in text to be set out vertically rather than to be presented in continuous prose. Thus, for example, readers prefer text set in the style of Figure 5/4b to that of Figure 5/4a, below. Note how, in Figure 5/4b, the text is aligned vertically, indented away from the 'bullet', and that it does not return to the left hand margin.

Summary

1. The argument in this chapter is that consistent spacing helps readers to perceive the organization and underlying structure of a piece of text.
2. Line-spacing can be used consistently throughout a text to separate and group related parts of the text.
3. Similarly, consistent word-spacing can also be used as a device for better displaying the structure of text.
4. Readers prefer text which has clear, consistent spacing to text which has not.

References

Hartley, J (1993) 'Recalling structured text: does what goes in determine what comes out?', *British Journal of Educational Technology*, 24, 2, 84–91.

Misanchuk, E A (1992) *Preparing Instructional Text: Document design using desktop publishing*, Englewood Cliffs, NJ: Educational Technology Publications.

Thompson, B (1988) *The Art of Typographic Design*, Yale: Yale University Press.

The Washburn College Bible (1980) New York: Oxford University Press.

Suggested further reading

Jandreau, S and Bever, T G (1992) 'Phrase-spaced formats improve comprehension in average readers', *Journal of Applied Psychology*, 77, 143–6.

Appendix: Style sheet for *Designing Instructional Text*

The final style sheet for this book included the following items and decisions:

- page size   246 mm x 189 mm

- margins
upper	14 mm
lower	17 mm
outer	21 mm
inner	16 mm

- column widths
main	101 mm
inner	46 mm
gutter	5 mm

- column depth   51 lines $\pm$ 2

- type-faces
chapter title	Galliard, bold
introductory summary	Galliard bold
body of the text	Sabon Roman
main headings	Galliard bold
running heads	Galliard Roman
secondary headings	Galliard Roman
tertiary headings	Galliard Roman
figure and table captions	Gill Sans Bold
references	Sabon Roman
index	Sabon Roman

- type-sizes
chapter title	28 point
introductory summary	9.5/11.5
body of the text	9.5/11.5
running heads	10/11.5
main headings	14/14
secondary headings	14/14
tertiary headings	12/12
examples in text	varies
figure and table captions	9.5/11.5
references and further reading	9.5/11.5
index	8.5/10.5

- inter-line feed (ie, base-line to base-line)
below chapter title	110 points
body of the text	11.5 points
above main headings	23 points
below main headings	11.5 points
above secondary headings	11.5 points
below secondary headings	5.75 points
above tertiary headings	11.5 points (para setting)

above tables and figures	24 points
below tables and figures	24 points
above end summary	24 points

The text is to be left-ranged text throughout.
Hyphenation is to be avoided.
There is to be a 'floating baseline' of plus/minus two lines.
Page numbers to be positioned top left and top right.
First page of each chapter to start on left or right hand page.

These decisions were made in advance of production of the text to ensure that the layout was consistent throughout it. This does not mean that these decisions (or rules) were never changed – but it does mean that a great deal of consideration was given before overriding them to meet special requirements.

Note: this final style sheet is not specific enough to be called a *template*. Templates are used when people fill text in to a particular format. Decisions concerning the page-size, layout and perhaps the sequence of items are pre-specified, as in a style sheet. These decisions appear on screen and the relevant textual material is slotted in as appropriate. Templates are useful when the text is of a standard format, for example, bills, letterheads, visiting cards, and possibly some worksheets and distance learning materials.

6 Writing instructional text

This chapter offers guidelines for writing instructional text. Here I consider issues such as organization, clarity and revision. The advantages of computer-aided writing and revising are also outlined.

It is convenient to distinguish between three – overlapping – stages in writing instructional text: planning, writing and revising.

The *planning* stage is concerned with making decisions about the scope and purpose of the document. Writers need to know who the document is for, how it is likely to be used, and what restrictions operate on them as writers of the document.

The *writing* stage is concerned with producing the document. It involves writing the appropriate text, organizing it clearly, and presenting it in a clear and simple language with appropriate illustrative materials.

The *revising* stage is concerned with editing the document, testing it with users and revising it on the basis of the results obtained. The aim of this stage is to improve the document – so editing, testing and rewriting are all positive procedures.

Although this chapter focuses mainly on writing, this does not mean that planning and revising are not important. In fact, as we shall see, writing processes are recursive, and writers do not proceed directly from one step to the next. Writers constantly shift back and forth from planning, writing and editing as they proceed.

In this chapter I have drawn together some guidelines on writing instructional text from the more technical research literature.
The purpose of providing these guidelines is to give suggestions which readers can consider when they are writing text. The aim is to indicate the kinds of choices available and the possible effects of making particular ones. Specific circumstances will necessitate more detailed consideration, and this may mean that some particular suggestions will not always be appropriate. Clearly, writing for children is different from writing for adults, and writing 'required' materials may be different from writing 'free-choice' ones. None the less, having these suggestions at hand may result in a better text. And, with desk-top publishing, it is now much easier to compare different ways of doing the same thing and to decide which one seems best.

Organizing text

There are a number of features that help readers find their way around a text. The design of some of these will be discussed in later chapters.

Here I shall make a few remarks about titles, summaries, headings and the sequencing of text.

Titles. Titles aim to describe the content of a text in the fewest words possible – but sometimes these are supplemented with a subtitle. Such succinct descriptions help to focus attention and expectations, and studies have shown that titles affect the readers' perception and interpretation of ambiguous text. However, it is to be hoped that instructional text will not be ambiguous. Thus one would hardly expect titles to have much effect on the comprehension of text of this kind – although they may aid later recall of what the text was about. Unfortunately, I know of no research on typographic variables connected with the setting of titles (eg, type-sizes, type-faces, weights, etc.) and none on the more interesting problems of using different title formats (eg, statements, questions, quotations).

Summaries. Summaries in text have different positions and roles. *Beginning* summaries tell the readers what the text is about, they help the readers to decide whether or not they want to read it, and they help the readers who do read it to organize their subsequent reading. *Interim* summaries draw together the argument so far, and indicate what is to come. *End* summaries list or review the main points made, and thus aid the recall of important points in the text. End summaries can use the more technical vocabulary introduced in the text: beginning summaries (as in this book) might not.

Summaries can be typeset in many different ways – in medium, bold or italic, in large or small type, boxed, etc. There is no research to my knowledge on the effect of such typographic variables in this context, although there is some indication that readers dislike journal abstracts set in a smaller type-size than the main body of the text.

Headings. Headings may be written in the form of questions, statements or (like here) with one- or two-word labels. Headings may be placed in the margin or in the body of the text.

In a series of experiments with secondary school children Mark Trueman and I investigated the role of different kinds of heading (questions versus statements) and their position (marginal versus embedded). We concluded that headings significantly aided search, recall and retrieval but that the position and the kinds of heading that we used had no significant effects with the texts that we employed. More studies still need to be carried out on factors such as:

- the nature of the text (technical versus semi-literary);
- the frequency of headings; and
- the typographic denotation of headings of different levels (primary, secondary, tertiary).

Questions. Questions may be interspersed in the text itself, or presented in a list at the end of a chapter to provide material for exercises. There is some indication that readers ignore questions given at the ends of chapters, so it might be more appropriate to consider how best they can be embedded in the text. It appears that factual questions, placed in a passage *before* paragraphs of relevant material, often lead to specific learning, whereas similar questions placed in the passage *after* the relevant content will sometimes lead to more general learning as well. The level of difficulty of these questions, too, may be important.

Some of our earlier research suggested that headings in the form of questions were particularly suitable for less-able readers, but our more recent (better designed) studies failed to confirm this. None the less, it might be important to consider headings in this form for certain texts.

Sequencing. There has been little research on the sequencing of sentences or paragraphs within instructional text, apart from work with programmed instruction and work with the design of forms. Some work with programmed instruction suggests that violations in natural sequences provide little difficulty for most readers but work with forms (see Chapter 10) suggests just the opposite. Here natural sequencing seems best. However, just what is a 'natural' sequence? Posner and Strike (1976) contrast 17 different ways to show that sequencing is not a simple matter, and Van Patten *et al* (1986) develop these issues further.

There are some situations, however, where we might all agree that the sequence used is unhelpful. Take, for example, this odd sequence of instructions I once found for using an electric razor:

1. To gain access to the heads for cleaning, press the button on the side of the appliance (see Fig. 4).
2. To remove the razor from its packaging...

Certainly readers find it easier to follow a sequence in which the events match the temporal order in which they occur. *Compare* 'Before the machine is switched on, the lid must be closed and the powder placed within its compartment', *with* 'The powder must be placed in its compartment and the lid closed before the machine is switched on'.

Sequencing lists. It is fairly common in instructional writing to find a sentence such as this:

Five devices which aid the reader are (i) skeleton outlines for each chapter, (ii) headings in the text, (iii) an end summary, (iv) a glossary for new technical terms, and (v) a comprehensive subject and author index.

However, as noted in Chapter 5, research suggests that readers prefer text which has such lists or numbered sequences spaced out and separated, rather than run-on in continuous text. My example would be better thus:

Five devices which aid the reader are:
- (i)   skeleton outlines for each chapter;
- (ii) headings in the text;
- (iii) an end summary;
- (iv) a glossary for new technical terms; and
- (v)   a comprehensive subject and author index.

This example also shows, however, how the use of the Roman numbering system can affect the layout: Arabic numbers – or letters of the alphabet – might be preferable. Another choice is the use of 'bullets' – thus:

Five devices which aid the reader are:
- skeleton outlines for each chapter;
- headings in the text;
- an end summary;
- a glossary for new technical terms; and
- a comprehensive subject and author index.

Arabic numbers are perhaps best when there is an order, or sequence in the points being made. Bullets seem more appropriate when each point is of equal value.

Signalling. Another way of making text organization more explicit is to use verbal 'signals'. Signals have been defined as 'non-content words that serve to emphasize the conceptual structure or organization of the passage'. Words and phrases such as *however*, *but*, or *on the other hand*, signal to the reader that some form of *comparison* is to be made. Similarly, words and phrases such as *first, second, three reasons for this are . . . , a better example, however, would be . . .* , signal the *structure of the argument* (and comparisons with subsections). Likewise, words and phrases such as *therefore, as a result, so that, in order to, because*, signal *causal* relationships.

Numbers in text. Numbers can also be used to signal the structure of text. As noted above, it is helpful when making a series of points to list and enumerate them. However, when presenting numerical data in text, prose descriptions often seem more comfortable than actual numbers. Everyday words that act as rough quantifiers, eg, 'nearly half the group', seem adequate for most purposes and are handled with reasonable consistency by most people.

Research has suggested that the following phrases can be used with confidence:

Numerical value to be conveyed	Suitable phrases
above 85%	almost all of . . .
60–75%	rather more than half of . . .
40–50%	nearly half of . . .
15–35%	a part of . . .
under 10%	a very small part of . . .

None the less, it may be better (or at least clearer for the reader) if more exact verbal equivalents of numbers are given. For example:

Numerical value to be conveyed	Suitable phrases
100%	all of...
75%	three-quarters of...
50%	half of...
25%	a quarter of...
0%	none of...

Verbal descriptions of probabilities are also more comfortable for most people than are actual probability statements. People are less consistent, however, in their interpretations of verbal descriptions of probability than they are in their interpretations of verbal descriptions of quantity. If precision is required, actual quantities can be given with a verbal quantifier. For example, one can say 'nearly half the group – 43 per cent – said...' or 'There was a distinct chance ($p < 0.06$) that...'.

Reference numbers. Paragraphing in text is often aided by the use of numbering systems. Such systems can be used to organize information in many different ways, eg, Section 1, 2, 3 or 1.01, 1.02, 1.03 etc.

There has been little research on the effectiveness of such systems. Many people undoubtedly feel that they are valuable – particularly for reference purposes. But such systems can be abused if they are overdone and they can lead to extraordinary confusion.

Figure 6/1

An example of a text with a multiple numbering system (page 10 of S100, Unit 26, © The Open University, reproduced with permission).

26. 1. 2 A modern coastal environment

The idea of interpreting the past in terms of the present sounds extremely simple, but there are many practical difficulties. An insight into the extent of these can be gained by considering the present-day environment from a geological point of view.

So you should now read the section in Chapter 13 of *Understanding the Earth* entitled 'environmental analysis - the beach' (pp. 180-5).

When you read this section, examine Figure 14 in Appendix 3 (p. 34), which summarizes information on the sediments and faunas of a modern beach. Plate A and TV programme 26 are about this area. *Make sure that you have examined Figure 14 thoroughly and have read pp. 180-5 of* Understanding the Earth *given above before viewing the television programme.* The post-broadcast notes will refer you to Appendix 3 which describes a 'geological model' of this stretch of coast and summarizes the sequence of 'rocks in the making' in this environment.

Figure 6/1 was provided by Robert Waller to give an illuminating example. He comments with regard to this material (taken from an Open University correspondence text) that such a chaotic use of numbering reflects a general confusion about its purpose.

Waller concludes his article on numbering systems with the following five guidelines for educational texts:

- Use numbers mainly for reference. Chapter, page and figure numbers are almost always perfectly adequate for continuous prose texts.
- Consider incorporating figure numbers, exercise numbers, and so on into the chapter numbering systems, particularly when there are too few figures for easy location or when too many different systems would cause confusion.
- Use arabic, not roman, numerals.
- Place page numbers near the fore-edge of the book so that it is easy to see them when flicking through.
- If in-text numbering has to be used, place the numbers in the margin rather than within the column.

Footnotes. To Waller's guidelines I would add one more: avoid the use of footnotes. Most footnotes can be incorporated in the text and excess material may be placed in an appendix, where it can be read by the interested reader. Footnotes can be difficult to typeset, and many publishers expressly forbid them. Certainly footnotes are often irritating to the reader (i) because they break up the reading flow[1], and (ii) because they seem so irresistible[2].

Text difficulty

Sentence length. Long sentences – such as this one – are difficult to understand because they often contain a number of subordinate clauses which, because of their parenthetical nature, make it difficult for readers to bear all of their points in mind and, in addition, because there are so many of them, make it harder for readers to remember the first part of the sentence when they are reading the last part. Long sentences overload the memory system: short sentences do not.

I once wrote 'As a rule of thumb, sentences less than 20 words long are probably fine. Sentences 20 to 30 words long are probably satisfactory. Sentences 30 to 40 words long are suspect, and sentences containing over 40 words will almost certainly benefit from rewriting.' Perceptive readers will notice that many sentences in this textbook contain more than 30 words – but at least they have been scrutinized!

Word length. Long words – like long sentences – also cause difficulty. It is easier to understand short familiar words than technical terms which

---

[1] by bringing you down here and making you find your way back
[2] see what I mean?

mean the same thing. If, for example, you wanted to sell *thixotropic* paint, you would probably do better to call it *non-drip*! One author on style quoted a letter writer in *The Times* who asked a government department how to obtain a book. He was 'authorized to acquire the work in question by purchasing it through the ordinary trade channels' – in other words, 'to buy it'. Concrete words and phrases are shorter and clearer than abstract ones. (This argument is developed further in Chapter 10.)

Paragraph lengths. Few researchers have commented on the effects of long chapters and long paragraphs. It would seem, other things being equal, that short chapters, and short paragraphs within them, will make a text easier to read. However, no doubt such procedures can be overdone.

Clarifying text. Generally speaking, text is usually easier to understand when:

1. Writers produce few sentences containing more than two subordinate clauses. The more subordinate clauses or modifying statements there are, the more difficult it is to understand a sentence. Consider, for example, the problems posed for an anxious student by this examination rubric: 'Alternative C: Answer four questions including at least one from at least two sections (1–5)'.
2. Writers use the active rather than the passive voice. Compare the active form, 'We found that the engineers had a significantly higher interocular transfer index than did the chemists' with the passive form, 'For the engineers, as compared with the chemists, a significantly higher interocular transfer index was found'.
3. Writers use positive terms (eg, more than, heavier than, thicker than) rather than negative ones (eg, less than, lighter than, thinner than). Compare 'The rain is heavier today' with 'The rain was lighter yesterday'.
4. Writers avoid negatives, especially double or treble ones. Negatives can often be confusing. For example, I once saw a label fixed to a machine in a school workshop which read, 'This machine is dangerous: it is not to be used only by the teacher'. Harold Evans provides another example. *Compare* 'The figures provide no indication that costs would have not been lower if competition had not been restricted' with 'The figures provide no indication that competition would have produced higher costs'. Negative qualifications *can* be used, however, for particular emphasis and for correcting misconceptions. Double negatives in imperatives (eg, 'Do not ... unless ...') are sometimes easier to understand than single ones.
5. Writers 'personalise texts'. In one study that Cathryn Brown and I conducted we compared two medical audiotapes. The first tape began:

    > Welcome to the Health Department's Medical Directory. This tape is about multiple sclerosis: what causes it, and what you can do about it.

The second tape began:

> Welcome to the Health Department's Medical Directory.
> My name is Nick and I want to tell you about multiple sclerosis. I am able to do this because I am suffering from the disease. In this tape I will tell you about what causes multiple sclerosis and what you can do about it.

Both tapes contained the same information but, while the first tape was formal, the second tape conveyed the information in a more personal way. Students listening to this tape recalled more information from it than they did from the first one.

Personalizing instruction, of course, can take many forms. It is possible to insert the appropriate names of people and places in computer-generated texts, and problems can be tailored to students' backgrounds (eg, the same mathematical problems can be presented in different contexts for nursing, teaching, psychology students, etc).

Measuring text difficulty. There are many readability formulas available that quantify and predict the difficulty of prose text. These formulas typically combine (usually with a constant) two main measures – average sentence-lengths and average word-lengths – to predict the difficulty of text. Thus, the longer the sentences and the more complex the vocabulary, the more difficult the text will be.

Many readability formulas can be calculated by hand. One of the simplest, the Gunning Fog Index, is as follows:

- take a sample of 100 words;
- calculate the average number of words per sentence in the sample;
- count the number of words with three or more syllables in the sample;
- add the average number of words per sentence to the total number of words with three or more syllables; and
- multiply the result by 0.4.

The result is the (American) reading grade level. To obtain a British equivalent of reading age it is conventional to add five, as a fifth-grade American pupil is normally 10 years old. (Note, however, that British schoolchildren have one extra year's schooling compared to American ones.)

A better known formula, but one which is harder to calculate by hand, is the Flesch Reading Ease (RE) formula. This is:

$$RE = 206.835 - 0.846 \; w - 1.015 \; s$$
where w = average number of syllables per 100 words
s = average number of words per sentence.
(In this case, the *higher* the RE score, the easier the text.)

The relationship between RE, difficulty and suggested reading ages is as follows:

Table 6/1

A table for calculating the reading difficulty of text based on the Flesch formula. Each cell gives the British reading age in years. (Table reproduced with permission of Aubrey Nicholls).

Average Number of Syllables Per 100 Words

Average Number of Words Per Sentence ↓

Words/Sentence	105	110	115	120	125	130	135	140	145	150	155	160	165	170	175	180	185	190	195
8											13	13	15	15	15	18	18	18	18
	9	9	9	10	10	11	11	12	12	12	14	14	17	17	17	21	21	21	21
10											13	13	13	15	15	18	18	18	18
	9	9	10	10	10	11	11	12	12		14	14	14	17	17	21	21	21	21
12											13	13	15	15	15	18	18	18	
	9	9	10	10	11	11	12	12	12		14	14	17	17	17	21	21	21	
14									13	13	13	15	15	18	18	18	18	18	
	9	10	10	10	11	11	12	12	14	14	14	17	17	21	21	21	21	21	
16									13	13	15	15	15	18	18	18	18		
	9	10	10	11	11	11	12	12	14	14	17	17	17	21	21	21	21		
18								13	13	13	15	15	18	18	18	18	18		
	10	10	10	11	11	12	12	14	14	14	17	17	21	21	21	21	21		
20								13	13	15	15	15	18	18	18	18			
	10	10	11	11	11	12	12	14	14	17	17	17	21	21	21	21			
22								13	13	13	15	15	18	18	18	18	18		
	10	10	11	11	12	12	14	14	14	17	17	21	21	21	21	21			
24							13	13	15	15	15	18	18	18	18				
	10	11	11	11	12	12	14	14	17	17	17	21	21	21	21				
26							13	13	15	15	18	18	18	18	18				
	10	11	11	12	12	12	14	14	17	17	21	21	21	21	21				
28						13	13	15	15	15	18	18	18	18					
	11	11	11	12	12	14	14	17	17	17	21	21	21	21					
30						13	13	15	15	18	18	18	18	18					
	11	11	12	12	12	14	14	17	17	21	21	21	21	21					
32					13	13	15	15	15	18	18	18	18	18					
	11	11	12	12	14	14	17	17	17	21	21	21	21	21					
34					13	13	15	15	18	18	18	18	18				College		
	11	12	12	12	14	14	17	17	21	21	21	21	21				or		
36				13	13	15	15	15	18	18	18	18	18				above		
	11	12	12	14	14	17	17	17	21	21	21	21	21						
38				13	13	15	15	18	18	18	18	18							
	12	12	12	14	14	17	17	21	21	21	21	21							
40			13	13	13	15	15	18	18	18	18	18							
	12	12	14	14	14	17	17	21	21	21	21	21							

RE value	Description of style	Required reading skill
90–100	Very easy	5th grade
80–90	Easy	6th grade
70–80	Fairly easy	7th grade
60–70	Standard	8–9th grade
50–60	Fairly difficult	10–12th grade
30–50	Difficult	13–16th grade
0–30	Very difficult	College graduate

To save effort and calculation, the chart shown in Table 6/1 can be used to calculate the British reading age for texts used in the United Kingdom

Today, with word-processing systems, it is now much easier to apply the more complex readability formulas. For example, the Style program of the IBM Xenith text-formatting system can be applied to text to provide four sets of readability data derived from four different formulas. When this program was run on the first 20 sentences of Chapter 1 in this book, the outcomes were as follows:

	Formula	British Reading Age
1.	Flesch	17 years
2.	Kincaid	15–16 years
3.	Auto	15–16 years
4.	Coleman-Liau	16 years

It can be seen that the predictions from the four formulas vary slightly but are reasonably consistent.

Readability formulas such as these have obvious limitations. Some short sentences are difficult to understand (eg, 'God is grace'). Some technical abbreviations are short (eg, 'DNA') but difficult for people unfamiliar with them. Some long words, because of their frequent use, are quite familiar (eg, communication). The order of the words, sentences and paragraphs is not taken into account, nor are the effects of other aids to understanding such as illustrations, headings, numbering systems and typographical layout. Also, most importantly, the readers' motivation and prior knowledge of the topic are not assessed. All of these factors affect text difficulty.

None the less, despite these problems, readability formulas can be useful tools for having a quick look at the likely difficulty of text that is being produced, and also for comparing the relative difficulty of two or more pieces of text.

Comparison studies of original and revised texts have shown advantages for more readable text in

- examination questions
- scientific papers
- school textbooks
- correspondence materials

- job aids
- medical instructions
- insurance policies
- legal documents, and even
- fairy tales! (Britton *et al.*, 1993)

Table 6/2 shows how the marks obtained on examination questions improve when the questions are made easier to understand.

Table 6/2

shows the percentage of correct responses given to original and revised multiple-choice questions asked in a pre-O level chemistry examination by approximately 6,000 pupils. Data reproduced with permission from Johnstone and Cassels (1978).

Original questions	% correct	Revised questions	% correct
Which one of the following requires a non-aqueous solvent to dissolve it? A Salt B Sugar C Sodium nitrate D Sulphur	34	Which one of the following requires a liquid other than water to dissolve it? A Salt B Sugar C Sodium nitrate D Sulphur	49
An element has only three isotopes of mass numbers 14, 16 and 17. Which one of the following could **not** be the atomic weight of the element? A 14.2 B 15.4 C 16.3 D 17.1	50	An element has only three isotopes of mass numbers 16, 16 and 17. Which one of the following could be the atomic weight of the element? A 11.7 B 13.9 C 15.1 D 17.2	62
The atomic weight of chlorine is usually quoted as 35.5. It is not a whole number despite the fact that protons and neutrons have very closely integral atomic weights because A Ions are present B Impurities are present C Unequal numbers of protons and neutrons are present D Isotopes are present	66	The atomic weight of chlorine is 35.5. Why is it not a whole number? A Ions are present B Impurities are present C Unequal numbers of protons are present D Isotopes are present	78

Difficult short sentences. It does not necessarily follow, of course, that passages written in short sentences and short words will always be better understood. Alphonse Chapanis (1965; 1988) provides many examples of short pieces of text that are difficult to understand. The one I like best is the notice that reads:

PLEASE
WALK UP ONE FLOOR
WALK DOWN TWO FLOORS
FOR IMPROVED ELEVATOR SERVICE

People interpret the notice as meaning 'to get on the elevator I must either walk up one floor, or go down two floors', or even 'to get on the elevator I must first walk up one floor and then down two floors'. When they have done this they find the same notice confronting them! What this notice means, in effect, is 'Please, don't use the elevator if you are only going a short distance'. Chapanis' articles are well worth studying. They are abundantly illustrated with short sentences that are hard to understand and (in some cases) potentially lethal.

Ambiguities. Many short (and indeed many long) sentences can turn out to be ambiguous. Consider 'Then roll up the three additional blankets and place them inside the first blanket in the canister'. Does this sentence mean that each blanket should be rolled inside the other, or that the three rolled blankets should be placed side by side and a fourth one wrapped around them? (An illustration would clarify this ambiguity.)

Ambiguities, or at least difficulties, often result from the use of abbreviations or acronyms (strings of capital letters which form words, eg, PLATO). I once counted over 20 such acronyms in a two-page text distributed by my university computer centre. Chapanis (1988) provides additional examples, also from the field of computing. The meanings of acronyms may be familiar to the writer but they need to be explained to the reader. Furthermore, readers easily forget what an author's abbreviations stand for when they are not familiar with the material.

Revising written text

There are numerous guidelines on how to write clear text and also on how to revise one's own text, or text written by someone else. In my own work with secondary school children I have used the guidelines given in Figure 6/2. These guidelines are based upon theoretical work conducted by psychologists and others on the nature of the writing process (see Hartley, 1992).

Several computer programs have now been developed to help writers produce both technical and conventional text. Many of these programs were originally designed to be run when the text had been written, in order to analyse it and to make suggestions for improvement. Today, however, we may expect writers to use such programs concurrently with their writing. Such programs point to potential difficulties and offer on-

Figure 6/2

Guidelines for revising text.

1. Read the text through.
2. Read the text through again but this time ask yourself:
   - What is the writer trying to do?
   - Who is the text for?
3. Read the text through again, but this time ask yourself:
   - What changes do I need to make to help the writer? How can I make the text clearer?
   - What changes do I need to make to help the reader? How can I make the text easier to follow?
4. To make these changes you may need:
   - to make big or *global* changes (eg, rewrite sections yourself); or
   - to make small or minor *text* changes (eg, change slightly the original text).

   You will need to decide whether you are going to focus first on global changes or first on text changes.
5. *Global* changes you might like to consider in turn are:
   - re-sequencing parts of the text;
   - re-writing sections in your own words;
   - adding in examples;
   - changing the writer's examples for better ones;
   - deleting parts that seem confusing.
6. *Text* changes you might like to consider in turn are:
   - using simpler wording;
   - using shorter sentences;
   - using shorter paragraphs;
   - using active rather than passive tenses;
   - substituting positives for negatives;
   - writing sequences in order;
   - spacing numbered sequences or lists down the page (as here).
7. Keep reading your revised text through from start to finish to see if you want to make any more global changes.
8. Finally, repeat this whole procedure some time after making your initial revisions (say, 24 hours) and do it without looking back at the original text.

screen advice. Figure 6/3 provides an illustration of the advice given to an author who had a 'dangling modifier' in her text.

One typical suite of such programs is *Grammatik 5*. The number of facilities available is currently being expanded but Table 6/3 lists some of them. One difficulty here is whether the novice writer can cope with all this information. Another appears to be that writers often need to understand sophisticated grammar to follow the advice offered by *Grammatik 5*!

Figure 6/3

The kind of advice given by *Grammatik 5*.

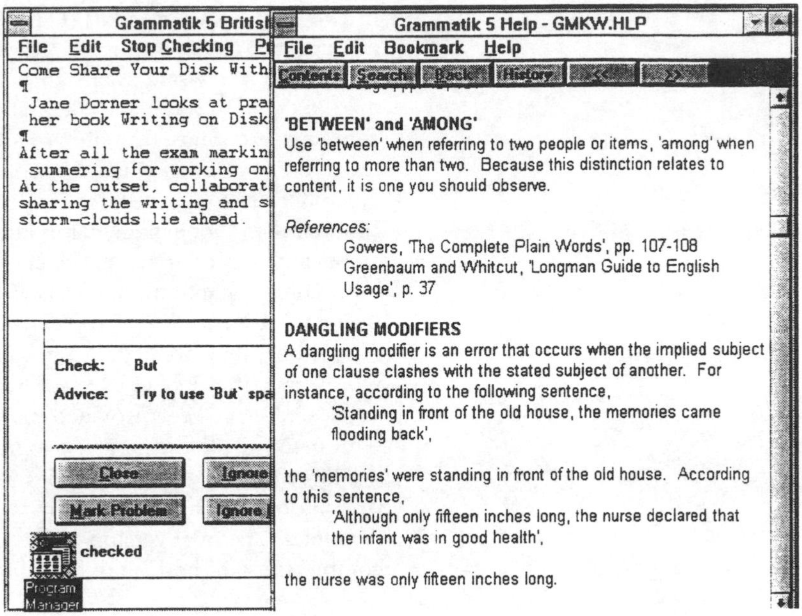
Grammatik 5 Britis
File Edit Stop Checking
Come Share Your Disk With
Jane Dorner looks at pra
her book Writing on Disk
After all the exam markin
summering for working on
At the outset, collaborat
sharing the writing and s
storm-clouds lie ahead.
Check: But
Advice: Try to use 'But' spa
Close
Ignore
Mark Problem
checked
Program Manager
Grammatik 5 Help - GMKW.HLP
File Edit Bookmark Help
Contents Search Back History << >>
'BETWEEN' and 'AMONG'
Use 'between' when referring to two people or items, 'among' when referring to more than two. Because this distinction relates to content, it is one you should observe.
References:
Gowers, 'The Complete Plain Words', pp. 107-108
Greenbaum and Whitcut, 'Longman Guide to English Usage', p. 37
DANGLING MODIFIERS
A dangling modifier is an error that occurs when the implied subject of one clause clashes with the stated subject of another. For instance, according to the following sentence,
'Standing in front of the old house, the memories came flooding back',
the 'memories' were standing in front of the old house. According to this sentence,
'Although only fifteen inches long, the nurse declared that the infant was in good health',
the nurse was only fifteen inches long.

Table 6/3

Examples of types of errors detected by *Grammatik 5*.

Grammatical errors	Mechanical errors	Stylistic errors
adjective errors	spelling errors	long sentences
adverb errors	capitalization errors	wordy sentences
article errors	double word	passive tenses
clause errors	ellipsis misuse	end of sentence prepositions
comparative/superlative use	end of sentence punctuation	split infinitives
double negative	incorrect punctuation	clichéd words/phrases
incomplete sentences	number style errors	colloquial language
noun phrase errors	question mark errors	Americanisms
object of verb errors	quotation mark misuse	archaic language
possessive misuse	similar words	gender specific words
preposition errors	split words	jargon
pronoun errors		abbreviation errors
sequence of tense errors		paragraph problems
subject-verb errors		questionable word usage
tense changes		

In 1984 I published a report (Hartley, 1984) on how useful one such set of computer-aided writing programs (*The Writer's Workbench*) had been to me in revising a particular article. I compared the suggestions made by nine colleagues in this respect with the suggestions made by the computer programs. The human and the computer aids to writing differed in two main ways. My colleagues were more variable than the computer programs: different colleagues picked on different things to comment on. None made comments in all of the (14) categories of comments that I derived in the enquiry. The computer programs were more thorough and more consistent than my colleagues – but this was over a narrower range of (six) categories. The programs picked up every misspelling, they drew attention to every sentence that was over 30 words long, they indicated that I had missed out a bracket – but did not say where – and they provided me with 85 suggestions for better wording! Thus the computer programs were excellent at doing the donkey work of editing: my colleagues excelled at using their knowledge to point out inconsistencies, errors of fact, and to suggest better examples. The final version of the article thus benefited from the combined use of both sources of information.

The use of computer programs to aid writing is increasing in our primary and secondary schools. A basic idea here is that just as the typewriter relieved the writer of thinking about the subgoal of producing legible text by hand, so the computer releases the writer from thinking about the other subgoals of transcription when writing. Composition becomes more enjoyable when it is easy to edit words, sentences and paragraphs. In addition, there is less fear of failure when the notion disappears that one has to produce a 'neat' handwritten copy the first or second time around. Whether or not learning to write with computers will change the nature of writing, or the ways in which we think, is an open question. However, it is one that is currently receiving much attention (see, for example, Hartley, 1993).

▼

Summary

1. Writing instructional text involves planning, writing and revising.
2. Guidelines are available for all of these three areas. Guidelines prompt readers to think about certain issues that they might otherwise forget, and they provide suggestions to consider.
3. Using summaries, headings, questions and lists helps to organize and sequence text. Using short sentences and simple vocabulary (usually) makes text easier to read.
4. Readability formulas offer crude guides to the difficulty of text: none the less they can provide useful indicators of the relative difficulty of different texts.
5. Computer-aided writing programs suggest how authors might improve the clarity of text. Such programs help authors with the technical details of writing but, at present, they do not help a great deal with decisions concerning content.

▲

References

Britton, B K, Gulgoz, S and Glynn, S. (1993) 'Impact of good and poor writing on learners: research and theory', in Britton, B K, Woodward, A and Binkley M (eds) *Learning from Textbooks*, Hillsdale, NJ: Erlbaum.

Chapanis, A (1965) 'Words, words, words', *Human Factors*, 7, 1, 1–17.

Chapanis, A (1988) ' "Words, words, words" revisited', *International Review of Ergonomics*, 2, 1–30.

Hartley, J (1984) 'The role of colleagues and text editing programs in improving text', *IEEE Transactions on Professional Communication*, PC-27, 1, 42–4.

Hartley, J (1992) 'Writing: a review of the research', in Hartley J (ed.) *Technology & Writing*, London: Jessica Kingsley.

Hartley, J (1993) 'Writing, thinking and computers', *British Journal of Educational Technology*, 24, 1, 22–31.

Johnstone, H and Cassels, J (1978) 'What's in a word', *New Scientist*, 73, 1103, 432–34.

Posner, G J and Strike, K A (1976) 'A categorisation scheme for principles of sequencing content,' *Review of Educational Research*, 46, 685–90.

Van Patten, B, Chao, C I and Reigeluth, C M (1986) 'A review of strategies for sequencing and synthesising information', *Review of Educational Research*, 56, 437–72.

Waller, R (1980) 'Notes on transforming No. 4: numbering systems in text', in Hartley, J (ed.) *The Psychology of Written Communication*, London: Kogan Page.

Suggested further reading

Armbruster, B B and Anderson, T H (1985) 'Producing "considerate" expository text: or easy reading is damned hard writing,' *Journal of Curriculum Studies*, 17, 247–74.

Britton, B K, Woodward, A and Binkley, M (eds) (1993) *Learning from Textbooks*, Hillsdale, NJ: Erlbaum.

Davison, A and Green, G (eds) *Linguistic Complexity and Text Comprehension: A re-examination of readability with alternative views*, Hillsdale, NJ: Erlbaum.

Garner, R *et al.* (1991) 'Interest and learning from text', *American Educational Research Journal*, 28, 3, 643–59.

Harrison, C (1980) *Readability in the Classroom*, Cambridge: Cambridge University Press.

Hartley, J (ed.) (1992) *Technology and Writing*, London: Jessica Kingsley.

Lockwood, F (1992) *Activities in Self-Instructional Texts*, London: Kogan Page.

Lorch, R, Lorch, E and Inman, W (1993) 'Effects of signaling topic structure on text recall', *Journal of Educational Psychology*, 85, 2, 281–90.

Moxey, L M and Sanford, A J (1993) *Communicating Quantities: A psychological perspective*, London: Erlbaum.

Penman, R (1990) 'Comprehensible insurance documents: plain English isn't good enough', Occasional Paper No. 14: Communication Research Institute of Australia, Acton, ACT 2600, Australia

The Plain English Campaign (1993) *The Plain English Story*, The Plain English Campaign, 15 Canal Street, Whaley Bridge, Stockport SK12 7LS.

Race, P (1992) *53 Interesting Ways to Write Open Learning Materials*, Bristol: Technical & Educational Services.

Renninger, K A, Hidi, S and Krapp, A (eds) (1992) *The Role of Interest in Learning and Development*, Hillsdale, NJ: Erlbaum.

Rook, K (1987) 'Effects of case-history versus abstract information on health attitudes and behaviors,' *Journal of Applied Social Psychology*, 17, 6, 533–53.

Sawyer, M H (1991) 'A review of research on revising instructional text', *Journal of Reading Behavior*, 23, 3, 307–33.

Schallert, D L, Alexander, P A and Goetz, E T (1988) 'Implicit instruction of strategies for learning from text,' in Weinstein, C (ed.) *Learning and Study Strategies: Issues in assessment, instruction and evaluation*, New York: Academic Press.

Sharples, M (ed.) (1992) *Computer Supported Collaborative Writing*, London: Springer-Verlag.

Steinberg, E R (ed.) (1991) *Plain Language: Principles and Practice*, Detroit: Wayne State University Press.

Tuman, M (1992) *Word Perfect: Literacy in the computer age*, London: Falmer Press.

US Department of Commerce, Office of Consumer Affairs (1984) *How Plain English Works for Business: Twelve case studies*, Washington, DC: US Government Printing Office.

Williams, N (1991) *The Computer, the Writer and the Learner*, London: Springer-Verlag.

7 Theory into practice

This chapter presents examples of instructional texts, first in their original states and then revised in the light of the previous discussion. The chapter includes examples to show the effects of changes in layout, changes in wording, and changes in both.

Figure 7/1

The original layout.

Example 1

Figure 7/1 shows the design used in a medical charter. This example is fabricated because the actual originators were not keen for me to provide a specific illustration from their text.

Every page in the original design of this charter presents a single 'right', such as the one shown here, and each occupies a centred rectangle in a blank page measuring 205mm x 205mm. The originators of the text believe that this uniform appearance of each page in their charter is important and that, as the letters are sufficiently large and the text sufficiently short, the uneven spacing between the words and the letters does not detract from legibility.

PATIENTS
HAVE THE
RIGHT   To
r e c e i v e
health   care
on the basis
of   clinical
n e e d,
regardless
of   ability
to pay.

To my mind this kind of design is not even appropriate for advertising literature, let alone the kind of text displayed here. The originators used justified text and, in order to make the text have straight left- and right-hand edges, they have varied the spaces between the words, and even the letters, to make the text fit.

I believe that the text would be easier to follow if it were printed thus:

Patients have the right to receive health care on the basis of clinical need, regardless of ability to pay.

Example 2

Figure 7/2a shows a page from a junior school science textbook, slightly reduced in size. The principal weakness of this page lies in the unsystematic way in which the illustrations, and the text which refers to them, are arranged on the page. Muddle of this kind is common in primary school textbooks (and in other materials). It shows a lack of rigour in the planning and specification of the work. Figure 7/2b shows a revised version.

Figure 7/2a

The original layout.

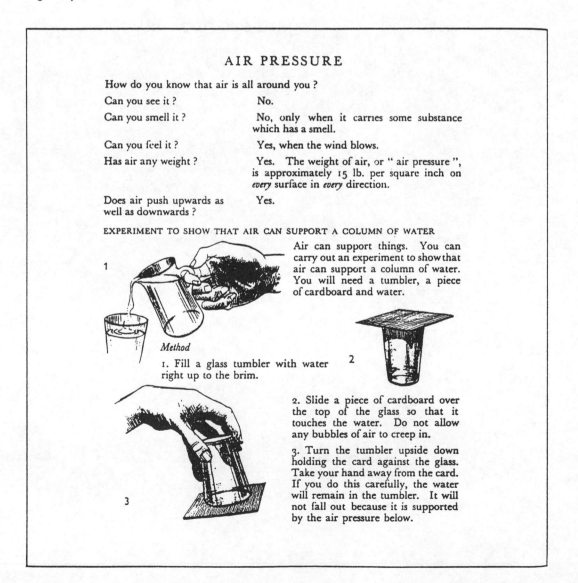

AIR PRESSURE

How do you know that air is all around you?

Can you see it?   No.

Can you smell it?   No, only when it carries some substance which has a smell.

Can you feel it?   Yes, when the wind blows.

Has air any weight?   Yes. The weight of air, or "air pressure", is approximately 15 lb. per square inch on *every* surface in *every* direction.

Does air push upwards as well as downwards?   Yes.

EXPERIMENT TO SHOW THAT AIR CAN SUPPORT A COLUMN OF WATER

1

Air can support things. You can carry out an experiment to show that air can support a column of water. You will need a tumbler, a piece of cardboard and water.

Method

1. Fill a glass tumbler with water right up to the brim.

2

2. Slide a piece of cardboard over the top of the glass so that it touches the water. Do not allow any bubbles of air to creep in.

3. Turn the tumbler upside down holding the card against the glass. Take your hand away from the card. If you do this carefully, the water will remain in the tumbler. It will not fall out because it is supported by the air pressure below.

3

Figure 7/2b

A revised layout.

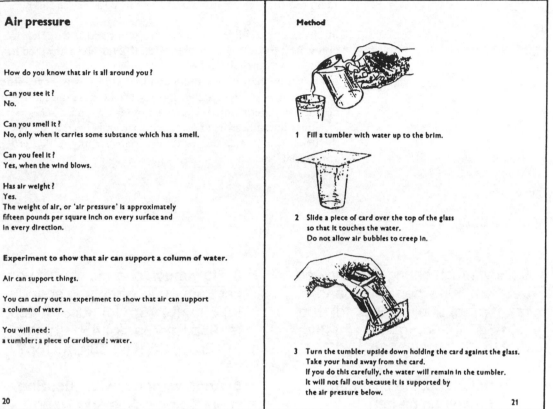

Air pressure

How do you know that air is all around you?

Can you see it?
No.

Can you smell it?
No, only when it carries some substance which has a smell.

Can you feel it?
Yes, when the wind blows.

Has air weight?
Yes.
The weight of air, or 'air pressure' is approximately
fifteen pounds per square inch on every surface and
in every direction.

Experiment to show that air can support a column of water.

Air can support things.

You can carry out an experiment to show that air can support
a column of water.

You will need:
a tumbler; a piece of cardboard; water.

20

Method

1   Fill a tumbler with water up to the brim.

2   Slide a piece of card over the top of the glass
    so that it touches the water.
    Do not allow air bubbles to creep in.

3   Turn the tumbler upside down holding the card against the glass.
    Take your hand away from the card.
    If you do this carefully, the water will remain in the tumbler.
    It will not fall out because it is supported by
    the air pressure below.

21

Example 3

Figure 7/3a shows a page from a primary school mathematics textbook. The main criticisms that can be made of this page are as follows:

1. In this example children first have to work across from left to right doing 5(a), (b), (c), etc. and then 6(a), (b), (c), etc. They then have to work *down*, doing 1, 2, 3 etc.
2. In answering questions 5 and 6 children are likely to have difficulty in keeping track of where they have got to because the sub-items are not clearly differentiated from each other by space.
3. The question indicators (1, 2, 3, etc.) are embedded in the text, and the items 1, 2, 3, etc. are not differentiated from each other by appropriate space.

Figure 7/3a

The original layout.

5 How much change should you get from 50p when you spend:
(a) 40p, (b) 20p, (c) 30p, (d) 10p,
(e) 45p, (f) 25p, (g) 42p, (h) 38p,
(i) 27p, (j) 34p, (k) 22p, (l) 17p?

1 Tom had 5p. He spent 3p. How much had he left?
2 Jim had 10p. He spent 4p. How much had he left?
3 Jean had 25p. She spent 6p on chocolate and 5p on sweets.
(a) How much did she spend?
(b) How much had she left?
4 John had 20p. He spent 9p on comics and 2p on sweets.
(a) How much did he spend?
(b) How much had he left?

6 How much change should you get from 100p when you spend:
(a) 50p, (b) 70p, (c) 80p, (d) 40p,
(e) 95p, (f) 75p, (g) 45p, (h) 25p,
(i) 42p, (j) 38p, (k) 58p, (l) 16p?

5 Anne went out with 30p. She spent 8p on cakes and 7p on lemonade.
(a) How much did she spend?
(b) How much had she left?
6 Shirley had 50p. She bought sweets for 12p and biscuits for 9p.
(a) How much did she spend?
(b) How much had she left?

Figure 7/3b

A revised layout.

Figure 7/3b shows the same information redesigned with these points in mind.

5 How much change should you get from 50p when you spend:

a 40p	e 45p	i 27p
b 20p	f 25p	j 34p
c 30p	g 42p	k 22p
d 10p	h 38p	l 17p

6 How much change should you get from 100p when you spend:

a 50p	e 95p	i 42p
b 70p	f 75p	j 38p
c 80p	g 45p	k 58p
d 40p	h 25p	l 16p

1 Tom had 5p. He spent 3p. How much had he left?

2 Jim had 10p. He spent 4p. How much had he left?

3 Jean had 25p. She spent 6p on chocolate and 5p on sweets.
   a How much did she spend?
   b How much had she left?

4 John had 20p. He spent 9p on comics and 2p on sweets.
   a How much did he spend?
   b How much had he left?

5 Anne went out with 30p. She spent 8p on cakes and 7p on lemonade.
   a How much did she spend?
   b How much had she left?

6 Shirley had 50p. She bought sweets for 12p and biscuits for 9p.
   a How much did she spend?
   b How much had she left?

Example 4

Ian Dennis (1975) found, in a study of hospital drug labelling systems on medicine bottles:

- a lack of standardization both between the hospitals and within the various types of medicine used by individual hospitals;
- poorly organized information, with little consistency in its order and terminology, and wide variations in the positioning of the elements on the labels;
- large type used for short names, and small type used for long names, irrespective of whether or not the kind of information being presented was the same;
- centred and justified typography which, together with a heavy use of capital letters and a haphazard mixing of type-styles and type-sizes, made the labels difficult to read.

These problems are illustrated in Figures 7/4a and 7/4b.

Figure 7/4a and 7/4b

These figures show designs of labels used in London hospitals.

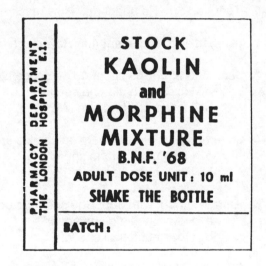

Dennis describes in his report how he and his colleagues set about designing:

● a standard range of label sizes and positions;
● a set of basic conventions governing the placing, spacing and grouping of information, and the grading of its importance;
● a restricted range of type-styles and type-sizes; and
● a consistent positioning of labels in relation to the side and front of the bottles and containers.

These changes are shown in Figure 7/4c. A study comparing the effectiveness of the new labels with the original ones showed that nurses made fewer errors locating medicines on shelves when they were labelled in the new manner.

Figure 7/4c

This figure shows a re-designed label. (These figures are reproduced with the permission of Ian Dennis.)

Kaolin and Morphine Mixture

Kaolin and Morphine Mixture BNF 68

Adult dose unit: 10ml

Shake the bottle
Do not use after

Stock : ward

Group Pharmacy
The London Hospital E1 1BB

Example 5

Figure 7/5a shows an extract from a complex piece of prose, slightly reduced in size, the clarity of which is not helped by its original typography. The original four-page document in fact contained seven

Figure 7/5a

The first page of the original notice sent out by the British Psychological Society. (Reproduced with permission of the Editors of the *Bulletin of the British Psychological Society*.)

THE BRITISH PSYCHOLOGICAL SOCIETY

(Incorporated by Royal Charter)

NOTICE IS HEREBY GIVEN that a Special General Meeting of the Society with be held in the Small Meeting House, Friends House, Euston Road, London NW1 on Saturday 26 October 1974 at 10.30 o'clock in the forenoon, when the following business will be transacted.

(1) To consider, and if thought fit, to approve the following SPECIAL RESOLUTIONS subject to obtaining the formal approval of the Privy Council:

A. That the Statutes of the Society be amended in the manner following, namely, by deleting the existing Statutes 4 and 8 and substituting the following new Statutes:

4. GRADUATE MEMBERS

(1) All persons who were elected Graduate Members of the old Institution and all persons who are elected as hereinafter provided shall be Graduate Members.

(2) A candidate for election as a Graduate Memeber:

    (a) shall satisfy the Council that he has one of the following qualifications and such higher qualifications as may be provided in the Rules: —

        (i) a university degree for which psychology has been taken as a main subject;

        or

        (ii) a postgraduate qualification in psychology awarded by an authority recognised by the Council;

        or

        (iii) such other qualification in psychology as the Council shall accept as not less than the foregoing;

        or

    (b) shall pass to the satisfaction of the Council such of the Society's examinations as may be required by the Rules.

(3) The Council may elect such eligible candidates to be Graduate Members as it thinks fit.

8. SUBSCRIBERS

(1) All persons who were elected Subscribers of the old Institution and who are elected as hereinafter provided shall be Subscribers.

(2) No technical qualification shall be required of a candidate for election as a Subscriber.

(3) A Subscriber shall be proposed in accordance with the provisions of the Rules.

levels of text. On this page there are six levels: there is a main item of business; special resolution A is part of this; statute 4 is part of resolution A; statute 4 has three parts; part 2 has subsections (a) and (b); and subsection (a) has parts (i), (ii) and (iii).

Such a text is difficult, if not impossible, to read when the spatial organization of the text is completely at variance with the sense.

Figure 7/5b shows a re-spaced equivalent (again slightly reduced in size) in which the hierarchical nature of the document has been clarified by using vertical and horizontal spacing more appropriately.

Figure 7/5b

A revised version.

The British Psychological Society
(Incorporated by Royal Charter)

Notice is hereby given that a Special General Meeting of the Society will be held in the Small Meeting House, Friends House, Euston Road, London NW1 on Saturday 26th October 1974 at 10.30 o`clock in the forenoon, when the following business will be transacted.

1st item of business   To consider, and if thought fit, to approve the following *Special Resolutions* subject to obtaining the formal approval of the Privy Council:

Resolution A   That the Statutes of the Society be amended in the manner following, namely, by deleting the existing Statutes 4 and 8 and substituting the following new Statutes:

Statute 4: Graduate Members

(1) All persons who were elected Graduate Members of the old Institution and all persons who are elected as hereinafter provided shall be Graduate Members.

(2) A candidate for election as a Graduate Member:

(a) shall satisfy the Council that he has one of the following qualifications and such higher qualifications as may be provided in the rules:-

(i) a university degree for which psychology has been taken as a main subject;

or

(ii) a postgraduate qualification in psychology awarded by an authority recognised by the Council;

Example 6

Figure 7/6a shows an extract from the first page of a three-page document. The problems with this page (as I see them) are:

- the setting of the paragraph numbers;
- the confusion between the paragraph numbers and numbers in the text (see 2.01);
- the use of justified text;
- the use of technical terms, long sentences and passive instructions.

Figure 7/6b shows the same text revised with these considerations in mind.

Figure 7/6a

The original text.

INSULATING GLOVES

1. GENERAL

1.01 This section covers the description, care and maintenance of insulating gloves provided for the protection of workmen against electric shock, and the precautions to be followed in their use.

1.02 This section has been reissued to include the D and E Insulating Gloves.

2. TYPES OF INSULATING GLOVES

2.01 All types of insulating gloves are of the gauntlet type and are made in four sizes: 9-1/2, 10, 11 and 12. The size indicates the approximate number of inches around the glove, measured midway between the thumb and finger crotches. The length of each glove, measured from the tip of the second finger to the outer edge of the gauntlet, is approximately 14 inches.

2.02 There are various kinds of insulating gloves. The original ones were just called Insulating Gloves. After that B, C, D and E Insulating Gloves were developed. As described below, the D Glove replaced the original Insulating Gloves and the E glove replaced the B and C Gloves.

2.03 **Insulating Gloves** are thick enough to eliminate the need for protector gloves and are intended for use without them. These gloves have been superseded by the D Insulating Gloves.

Figure 7/6b

A revised version.

INSULATING GLOVES

1.0   General

1.1   This section describes how to care for
and maintain the insulating gloves
that will protect you from electric shocks.

1.2   The section has been revised to include
the D and E Insulating Gloves.

2.0   Types of Insulating Gloves

2.1   All insulating gloves are made
in the gauntlet style.
There are four sizes: 9½, 10, 11, 12.
The size indicates the approximate number
of inches around the glove across the palm.
Each glove is about 14 inches long
from the bottom of the gauntlet to the top
of the second finger.

2.2   There are various kinds of insulating gloves.
The first kind were originally just called
Insulating Gloves.
After that the B, C, D and E Insulating Gloves
were developed.
As described below, the D Glove replaced the
original insulating gloves, and the E glove
replaced the B and C gloves.

2.3   So **Insulating Gloves** have now been replaced
by D Insulating Gloves.
(Insulating Gloves could be worn without
protector gloves.)

Example 7

Figure 7/7a shows extracts from a current Act of Parliament in the UK and Figure 7/7b shows a revised version. These figures are reproduced by courtesy of Martin Cutts. Cutts (1993) describes the changes made to revise the Act – changes in language, typography and structure.

Figure 7/7a

Extracts from the original document.

Parts of the original Act from which the proposed Act, opposite, is derived

---

An Act to provide for rights to cancel certain agreements about timeshare accommodation.

1   (7) This Act applies to any timeshare agreement or timeshare credit agreement if—

(a) the agreement is to any extent governed by the law of the United Kingdom or of a part of the United Kingdom, or

(b) when the agreement is entered into, one or both of the parties are in the United Kingdom.

12   (4) This Act shall have effect in relation to any timeshare agreement or timeshare credit agreement notwithstanding any agreement or notice.

4.—(1) Sections 2 and 3 of this Act do not apply where, in entering into the agreement, the offeree is acting in the course of a business.

13   (2) This Act shall come into force on such day as may be prescribed.

13   (3) This Act extends to Northern Ireland.

1   (5) In this Act "timeshare credit agreement" means, subject to subsection (6) below, an agreement, not being a timeshare agreement—

(a) under which a person (referred to in this Act as the "creditor") provides or agrees to provide credit for or in respect of a person who is the offeree under a timeshare agreement, and

(b) when the credit agreement is entered into, the creditor knows or has reasonable cause to believe that the whole or part of the credit is to be used for the purpose of financing the offeree's entering into a timeshare agreement.

(6) An agreement is not a timeshare agreement or a timeshare credit agreement if, when entered into, it may be cancelled by virtue of section 67 of the Consumer Credit Act 1974.

(8) In the application of this section to Northern Ireland—

(a) for the reference in subsection (2)(a) above to section 29(1) of the Caravan Sites and Control of Development Act 1960 there is substituted a reference to section 25(1) of the Caravans Act (Northern Ireland) 1963, and

12   (6) In this Act—

"credit" includes a cash loan and any other form of financial accommodation,

"notice" means notice in writing,

Figure 7/7b   c20   **Clearer Timeshare Act 1993** section 1

A revised version.

■ INTRODUCTION

1 What this Act does; when and where it applies

1.1 This Act gives a customer the right to cancel a timeshare agreement or timeshare credit agreement. Later sections explain how and when this may be done.

1.2 This Act applies to an agreement if:

(a) the customer is acting as a private individual when entering into the agreement;

(b) the seller or lender is acting in the course of a business when entering into the agreement; and

(c) at least one of the parties is in the United Kingdom when entering into the agreement, or the agreement is to some extent governed by the law of the United Kingdom or of a part of the United Kingdom.

1.3 The parties may not prevent this Act applying to an agreement.

1.4 This Act comes into force on a day to be prescribed.

1.5 This Act extends to Northern Ireland.

2 Meaning of words

2.1 The meanings of certain common words in Acts, such as 'person', 'summary' and 'writing', are given in the Interpretation Act 1978[1]. In addition, in this Act, whenever the following terms are used they have the meanings given here unless the context indicates otherwise.

Affirm means that the customer takes a significant action which shows that he or she considers the agreement to be in force.

Caravan means the same as in section 29(1) of the Caravan Sites and Control of Development Act 1960[2] when applying this Act to Great Britain, and the same as in section 25(1) of the Caravans Act (Northern Ireland) 1963[3] when applying this Act to Northern Ireland.

Credit includes a cash loan and any other form of financial support.

Customer means someone who, as a private individual, agrees to pay for a timeshare property through a timeshare agreement. As to a time before the agreement is entered into, this meaning includes someone who becomes the customer.

Lender means a person who, in the course of a business, provides or agrees to provide credit to or for a customer through a timeshare credit agreement.

Notice means notice in writing.

---

[1]1978 c30   [3]1963 c17(NI)   3
[2]1960 c62

Redish (1979) makes the following assertions about legal drafting:

1. People without legal training have to read and understand many legal documents.
2. Many legal documents cannot be read and understood by a lay person.
3. Much legal writing is unintelligible even to lawyers.
4. Tradition (not necessity) – and a lack of understanding of the audience – are the major reasons that legal language is so obscure.
5. Legal language can be made clear without losing its precision.

Since the interpretation of legal text can hang upon a comma (and full stops seem sparse) there is considerable opposition by the legal profession to changes of the kind advocated by these authors. The issues are well discussed by Cutts (1993) and in the Law Reform Commission of Victoria's (1987) Report, *Plain English and the Law*.

Summary

1. This chapter has shown how changes in layout and changes in wording can markedly affect the appearance of instructional text.
2. Whether these changes have actual effects on comprehension is a matter for evaluation. This particular issue is discussed in Chapter 14.

References

Cutts, M (1993) *Unspeakable Acts: Clarifying the language and typography of an Act of Parliament*, Words at Work, 69 Bings Road, Whaley Bridge, Stockport SK12 7ND.

Dennis, I (1975) 'The design and experimental testing of a hospital drug labelling system', *Programmed Learning and Educational Technology*, 12, 88-94.

Hartley, J and Burnhill, P (1976) 'Explorations in space: a critique of the typography of BPS publications', *Bulletin of the British Psychological Society*, 29, 97–107.

Hartley, J (1982) 'Designing instructional text', in Jonassen, D (ed.) *The Technology of Text*, Englewood Cliffs, NJ: Educational Technology Publications.

Law Reform Commission of Victoria (1987) *Plain English and the Law*, 160 Queen Street, Melbourne, Victoria 3000, Australia.

Redish, J (1979) 'How to draft more understandable legal documents', in MacDonald, D A (ed.) *Drafting Documents in Plain Language*, New York: Practising Law Institute (Handbook A4-3034).

Suggested further reading

Clare, C H and Gudjonsson, G (1992) *Devising and Piloting an Experimental Version of the 'Notice to Detained Persons'*, The Royal Commission on Criminal Justice: Research Report No. 7, London: HMSO.

Cutts, M and Maher, C (1981) 'Simplifying DHSS letters and forms', *Information Design Journal*, 2, 1, 28–32.

Hartley, J (1993) 'Communicating in print', in Trent, D and Reed, C (eds) *Promotion of Mental Health, Vol. 2*, Aldershot: Ashgate Publishing.

Kern, R P, Sticht, T G, Welty, D and Hauke, R N (1976) *Guidebook for the Development of Army Training Literature*, Alexandria, VA: Human Resources Research Organization.

One Book/5 Ways: The publishing procedures of five university presses, Los Altos, Ca: William Kaufmann Inc, 1977.

Penman, R (1993) 'Unspeakable acts and other deeds: a critique of plain legal language, *Information Design Journal*, 7, 2, 121–31.

8 Diagrams and illustrations

This chapter discusses research on the functions and effectiveness of diagrams and illustrations. I draw attention to the importance of the positioning and the labelling of such materials. In addition I discuss the problems of using additional colours.

In this text I have so far been discussing signs. Words, numbers and illustrations are all signs, but they are signs of different sorts. (Strictly speaking they are all 'sign-carriers', since the signs, or meanings, come from the reader.)

It is conventional to classify signs as being either *iconic* or *digital*. An iconic sign is one that resembles in some way the thing that it stands for. Photographs, drawings and illustrations in general are thus iconic signs. A digital sign need not resemble its referent in any way. Words, numbers, semaphore signs and the Morse code are all examples of digital signs. To interpret and understand the sign, the receiver must know the code. Sometimes, of course, iconic and digital sign systems are combined, as in text with illustrations, illustrations with captions, symbols which use explanatory labels (see Figure 8/1) and, of course, diagrams which depict structures and processes. The research shows that children and adults have difficulties in interpreting complex diagrams, particularly 'cross-sectional' and 'flow-process' ones.

Figure 8.1

Traffic signs provide examples of iconic and digital signs and also combinations of the two.
(1) Road works: iconic.
(2) Ford: digital.
(3) Axle weight limit: iconic and digital.

(1) (2) (3)

The functions of illustrative materials

Book authors and designers need to be aware of the various functions that are best fulfilled by different sorts of sign. Twyman (1979) has put forward a comprehensive classification scheme for this purpose, but here I shall only give a brief summary of the research findings in this area. (Such a summary, of course, provides only generalities which may not apply in every specific case and for all types of reader.)

It appears that diagrams and illustrations are interesting in their own right – thus they may *attract* or *distract* the reader. Words, on the other hand, are not particularly interesting as things in themselves – it is the ideas conveyed by the words that matter.

Illustrations are good for conveying concrete images (eg, a picture of an elephant may be 'worth a thousand words'). Diagrams are good for conveying structures and processes. Words are good for conveying abstract ideas and for communicating concepts *which have already been learned*. (For example, the word 'mammal' is probably worth several pictures.) Words can convey propositional concepts such as 'would be', 'might be' and 'should be' better than diagrams and illustrations.

If the information can be readily conveyed in words, then there may be no need for pictures. Conversely, if the information can be readily conveyed in a picture, then there may be no need for text. Diagrams and illustrations can be a good way of avoiding technical jargon. Thus one can argue that Figure 8/2 is a more effective way of communicating the instruction, 'See that the sliding dog associated with the reverse drive bevel is rotating freely before tightening the long differential casing'.

Figure 8/2

(Reproduced with permission of Patricia Wright.)

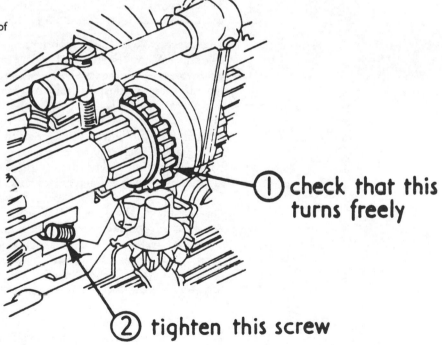

Illustrations are useful for conveying visual concepts (eg, what the Taj Mahal looks like) and spatial concepts (eg, the relative size of objects), although, in some cultures, two-dimensional representations of three-dimensional objects cause some difficulty. Temporal concepts can be translated into visual ones (clock faces, musical notes, time-charts, etc.), but such translations of time into space involve conventions which must be learned. Authors must either teach the code or be sure their readers know it.

Illustrations and diagrams are good for conveying ideas that have to be considered simultaneously – they allow learners to make multiple discriminations easily. Words, on the other hand, are possibly better for conveying ideas that have to be treated sequentially: thus words may be more important when the order in which the ideas are encountered is critical (eg, in reading a poem or in following a set of instructions). However, the use of cartoon strips for instruction shows the value of combining words and pictures.

One approach to assessing the effectiveness of diagrams and illustrations has been to consider them in terms of their functions. Some authors have suggested, for instance, that diagrams and illustrations may fulfil one or more of the following roles in instructional text:

- An affective role   – enhancing interest and motivation
- An attentional role – attracting and directing attention
- A didactic role   – facilitating learning by explaining or showing something that it is difficult to convey solely in words
- A supportive role   – enhancing the learning of less-able readers
- A retentional role   – facilitating long-term recall.

The didactic role is clearly important as far as instructional text is concerned. Many research studies have attempted to examine the effectiveness of this didactic role of illustrations. Clearly in such studies there are a large number of variables to consider, and at first sight it seems difficult to draw any general conclusions. Researchers have worked with different kinds of text (from children's books to technical manuals), used different kinds of illustrative materials (from line-drawings to coloured photographs), studied different groups of readers (from young to old, with high and low ability) and measured different things with different kinds of measuring techniques (from factual recall to drawing).

One recently developed statistical technique, however, allows researchers to pool together all of the studies on one particular topic and to look for average overall effects. Levie and Lentz (1982) used this approach with over 40 studies to consider the didactic role played by illustrations. These authors first found that they had to distinguish between three sources of information in illustrated text. These were:

1. Information provided only in the text;
2. Information provided only in the illustration(s); and
3. Information provided in both the illustrations and the text.

They then asked (from the results of the pooled studies) whether or not the illustrations aided the recall of information from all three sources. The results were surprisingly clear. Levie and Lentz found (overall) that there were marked effects for condition 3, ie, the recall of *text that was illustrated*. Text that was not illustrated (condition 1) and information that was illustrated but not discussed in the text (condition 2) did not fare nearly so well.

Thus it appears that pictures have an additive function in instructional text: they aid the recall of the textual material that they illustrate, but they do not really help the recall of the non-illustrated text.
These generalized conclusions have been largely supported by more recent research (see Misanchuk, 1992).

Levie and Lentz particularly mention the work of Francis Dwyer in their article. Dwyer has carried out over 100 studies in this field and his work is important because:

1. He has varied the types of illustration he has used;
2. He has varied the kinds of test he has used to measure their effectiveness; and
3. He has varied the media and conditions that he has used in his experiments.

Dwyer experimented with a 2,000-word passage on the human heart and eight types of illustration. These eight types were chosen to represent a continuum of realism as follows:

- simple line drawings (black and white)
- simple line drawings (coloured)
- detailed and shaded drawings (black and white)
- detailed and shaded drawings (coloured)
- photographs of a model (black and white)
- photographs of a model (coloured)
- realistic photographs (black and white)
- realistic photographs (coloured).

Control groups read the passage without any illustrations.

The tests Dwyer used were:

- A *drawing* test: participants were provided with a list of specific terms and asked to draw and label a diagram of the heart appropriately.
- A 20-item multiple-choice *identification* test: participants were asked to identify numbered items on a drawing of the heart.
- A 20-item multiple-choice *terminology* test: participants were required to demonstrate knowledge of specific terms and concepts.
- A 20-item multiple-choice *comprehension* test: participants were required to demonstrate a thorough understanding of the heart, its parts and its internal functioning.
- An *overall* test. Here a score was arrived at based on scores obtained on all of the tests listed above.

Experiments using these materials and tests were conducted with various media – prose text, workbooks, programmed instruction, tape-slides, film, television, etc. – and with learners who varied in age, ability, motivation and prior knowledge, to list just some of the variables.

Dwyer's findings were many and various, but his major findings were as follows:

1. There was no relationship between the test scores and the realism of the illustrations.
2. Different results were found with different tests: thus participants with illustrations did best on the drawing test, next best on the identification test, next the terminology test, and worst on the comprehension test. On this latter test they did not perform better than participants in control groups without illustrations.
3. Different results were found with different media. Simple line-drawings, for instance, were more effective with paced media (slides and television) whereas more detailed illustrations were more effective with self-paced media (printed text and programmed instruction).
4. Colour did not prove to be an effective device for all the tests and media: in the text presentations, however, colour did prove useful.

Dwyer has presented many more findings than these and more detailed accounts can be found elsewhere (Dwyer, 1972; 1976; 1987). The findings are, of course, restricted to the narrow range of materials used and the quality of their presentation. I have reported them here to illustrate the complexity of the task of assessing the effectiveness of illustrations.

Positioning and labelling diagrams and illustrations

There has been little satisfactory research on the positioning of illustrative materials in relation to the text. Like tables and graphs, illustrations are frequently put at the top or the bottom of a page without reference to where they are mentioned in the text.
Often, because of their size, they may be positioned on a following page. Obviously, it is not always easy to position illustrations directly after their first textual reference, especially if the illustrations are large and frequent and the text is minimal (as I have often found in preparing this book). Nonetheless, one might imagine that readers would prefer an illustration to appear immediately after its first textual reference than to have it positioned inconsistently in this respect. It is for this reason that I have sometimes completed a subsection of a chapter in this text with its illustrations on one page and then started a new subsection with its illustrations on the next one.

The positioning of illustrative materials is important because of their didactic and attentional roles. If such materials are divorced from the text then readers are less likely to look at them or to look at them for less time. One way to focus attention on such materials is to refer to them directly in the text (using such phrases as 'See Figure 1').
Another way is to label different parts of the illustration. A third way is to use captions.

Jones *et al.* (1984) argue that many diagrams are difficult to understand because there is no underlying organization to their labels. Often the reader has no idea where to start reading the labels or where to go in moving from one label to another. Jones *et al.* argue that labels should be chunked. Chunking involves grouping related labels under appropriate headings (see Figure 8/3) which, according to them, has a marked effect upon comprehension and recall.

Figure 8/3

A diagram with grouped or 'chunked' labels

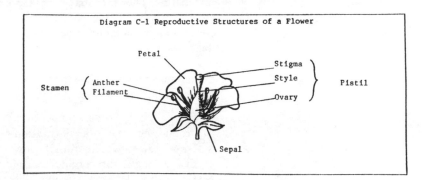

Curran (1978) reported the results from a study of labels or 'call-outs'. He investigated, among other things:

1.   The number of labels on two technical illustrations.
2.   The sequence of labels: they were presented either sequentially or in a random order in the illustrations.

Navy personnel were required (i) to locate parts on the diagram given a particular label, and (ii) to identify parts marked on the diagram. The results suggested that as the number of labels increased from 10 to 62, search time increased by a factor of three or four when the labels were presented in a random sequence. Curran suggested that if there were more than ten labels it would be better to number them in sequence. A point to consider here, of course, is whether or not the accompanying text also discusses the relevant items in sequence.

Labels and captions need to be presented in a consistent manner throughout the text, and thus their positioning is important too. Centred captions, for instance, vary their starting point from the left-hand margin according to the length of the caption. A simple caption (eg, 'Figure 10') might 'get lost' from the readers' point of view if it is centred and if all the other captions are lengthy and they start at the left hand margin.

Fitting illustrations and diagrams to the page

One of the difficulties of including illustrative materials in instructional text is that of deciding on their size. Usually, in a book of this kind, the problem is one of knowing how much space a particular illustration will take up. Often the original illustrations (which are being taken from another source) are too large, but reducing their size may make them difficult to read. Cropping, or focusing on particular parts of the illustration may help.

In a book of this kind, with its underlying grid, the procedures for deciding on the size of an illustration are relatively straightforward. All the tables and figures in this book start from either the inner or the text margin. They then may extend as far to the right as the information area allows, but they need not fill it. A decision then has to be made concerning the amount of vertical space required to insert an illustration.

To determine how much vertical space (in terms of units of line-feed) one needs to allow for an illustration, one can do the following:

- Place a piece of tracing paper over the illustration. Draw a rectangle around the area of the illustration that you wish to include.
- Draw a diagonal line from the lower left to the upper right corner of this rectangle, and continue beyond the rectangle if necessary.
- Decide how far you want your illustration to extend horizontally in your text. (This may be more or less than the picture you are working with.)
- Mark off this dimension along the baseline of your rectangle from its left hand corner.
- Draw a vertical line from this point until it joins the diagonal.
- Reduce or increase slightly the length of this vertical line until it is a precise number of units of line-feed.
- Add in the appropriate number of line-feed units for the space above the picture, for the space below it, for the caption, and for the space below that.
- The total number of line-feed units is the amount of space that you have to leave before the text starts again.

Scanners.   Today, several desk-top publishing systems and some personal computers allow one to use scanners to take illustrative materials and scan them directly into the text you are working with. It would appear then that sizing is not an issue, but you still need to decide on the depth of the figure in terms of an exact number of lines of text. An illustration, once it is scanned in, can be enlarged or reduced to fit the page layout, and sometimes changed and treated in the same way as other text. Three kinds of scanners are currently available: sheet-feed, flat-bed and hand-held.

Good quality scanners obviously have advantages. Misanchuk (1992) notes, 'Scanners are a godsend for people who cannot draw'. But there are problems too. Scanners may not be advisable for the reproduction of illustrations or photographs that have several different shades of grey (or colours). The quality of the scanned image in the document itself is also dependent upon the quality of the output device used to print it: 600, 1250 or 2500 dpi (dots per inch) laser printers produce much better results than 300 dpi ones. Finally, if the illustrations that are scanned vary in their original quality, then the output may look amateurish.

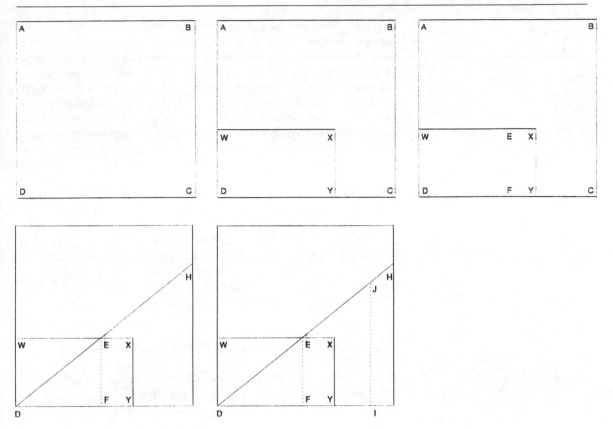

Figure 8/4

A procedure for determining the amount of space to be taken up in the text by a diagram or illustration.

(1) Tracing paper ABCD.
(2) Tracing paper over illustration WXYD.
(3) Illustration cropped to WEFD.
(4) Diagonal drawn from D through E to H.
(5) Vertical line drawn from I to J.

> Measure D to I gives the width.
> Measure I to J gives the height.
> I to J must be calculated in units of line-feed.
> Additional units of line-feed are needed for captions, and space above and below the illustration.

Clip art. Some commercial companies produce books of illustrations, cartoons, borders, logos, diagrams, etc., which are freely available for copying. Such 'clip art' can be pasted or scanned into the text. It is important, of course, not to use such materials arbitrarily, and to consider carefully what they add to the text. Clip art does allow you to illustrate your text, but often such materials do not match exactly what you want. It is probably better to avoid inappropriate material which will distract the learner. However, a number of companies now also produce *electronic clip art* and this does allow you to modify their original materials.

Copyright. Clearly, reproducing or scanning in someone else's text or illustrations without permission infringes the rules of copyright. Permission should be sought from the copyright holder (usually the author or the publisher) for the reproduction of lengthy pieces of text (say 15 lines or more) and for all illustrative materials, including tables and graphs. Such permission should also be acknowledged in the text. Clip art (electronic or otherwise) has an advantage here in that it is copyright-free, although one might be advised to read the small print carefully.

Pictures and procedural instructions

Step-by-step pictures and their captions are a common enough instructional device, and there is a small body of research on their design (see, for example, Morrell and Park, 1993). Figure 8/5 provides a typical

Figure 8/5

An example of a visual aid to help a procedural task. (Figure reproduced with permission from *Mending Things in Pictures*, Wolfe Publishing Ltd, 1976.)

replace ceramic wall tile

1   A tile which has been badly broken can be picked out piece by piece to leave a neat square to be filled.

2   A really hard blow may have damaged the plaster underneath. This must be repaired with filler.

3   Tile adhesive is applied using a spreader comb and the tile pushed into place level with surrounding tiles.

4   After a day, the gaps can be filled with tile grout. When this is dry, polish with a newspaper.

5   Do not try to remove a tile in one piece because you will probably break adjacent ones. Break it!

6   A tip when mounting accessories on a wall and tiles need to be drilled. A strip of sticky tape will stop the masonry drill tip from wandering.

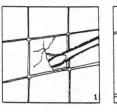
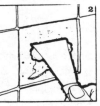

example where the spatial layout represents a temporal sequence. The instructions shown in Figure 8/5 seem clear but perhaps they might be better if the captions were placed appropriately beneath each picture. Furthermore, it might be helpful to repeat before each task the general instructions given in the preface of this instruction manual – as readers will hardly refer to it each time they use the text. These instructions, incidentally, are:

- Read the appropriate section carefully, right through before you start.
- Take careful note of any warning in the text.
- When doing a job read the individual stage caption in relation to the illustration to which it refers. Do not simply follow the pictures or skim the text.

What limited research there is on the use of pictures and diagrams to aid procedural tasks is somewhat confusing but it does suggest that simple, realistic and text-relevant illustrations help in the performance of procedural tasks. An early study by Booher (1975), for instance, compared the following types of instruction for three procedural tasks:

1. text only
2. pictures only
3. mainly text (but with supporting pictures)
4. mainly pictures (but with supporting text)
5. text (with pictures showing the same thing)
6. pictures (with text describing the same thing).

Booher found that Condition 4 (mainly pictures but with supporting text) and Condition 6 (pictures with text describing the same thing) were the most successful for all three procedural tasks. Somewhat similar findings were reported in an unpublished study by Jonathan Hawley – one of my undergraduate students. Hawley found in a knot-tying task that a sequence of photographs with instructions on the reverse was more effective than was the same sequence with instructions printed directly above the photographs. Hawley attributed this to the fact that the participants with the photographs with instructions on the reverse were not distracted by the instructions, and only referred to them if they wished.

One problem here (which is common to all studies with illustrative materials) is that some materials may be more effective than others. How far does the way in which a diagram or illustration is actually drawn affect learning? Relatively little research has been done on this problem, but work by Szlichcinski (1984) did show that alternative drawings of the same procedure produced different effects.

Finally in this section I shall comment briefly on the use of comic strips or cartoons in instruction. Clearly the affective role of instructions is to the fore in comic strips: their aim being to attract and motivate less-able learners (see Figure 8/6). Often cartoon strips are used to present a

Figure 8/6

Comic-strip cartoons can be an effective way of communication – but care still needs to be taken over their design. (Figure reproduced from the pamphlet *Good Health*, with permission of the Health Education Council.)

simplified form of instruction, but there has been little research on their effectiveness in this respect. Some variations that offer themselves for research seem to be:

- upper- versus lower-case dialogue
- balloon speech versus boxed speech
- the amount of text per balloon
- the size of print
- the integration of cartoons with conventional text, etc.

The general picture that emerges from studies of text with cartoon embellishments is that cartoons often enhance motivation, but they do not often increase comprehension.

What are the functions of colour in printed text?

Colour – like illustrations – is used in the provision of instructional materials for two rather different purposes. Colour can be used functionally to aid the instruction, or for aesthetic and motivational reasons.

Most people seem to agree that coloured illustrations are desirable from a *motivational* point of view, although the research suggests that the motivational effect of pictorial illustrations varies greatly with the age, the intelligence and the education of the reader. Younger and less intelligent children pay more attention to illustrations than do older, more intelligent ones.

Some researchers, however, have gone as far as to suggest that the prime function of most coloured illustrations in textbooks is to make the product more marketable. They argue that much of the pictorial material to which children are exposed (particularly in young children's early reading books) is designed more to reflect adult tastes than the learning requirements of the children.

A prime example of the functional use of colour is that provided by the well-known map of the London Underground system. Here several different colours are used, each to denote a separate route. It is often suggested that such a functional use of colour is a useful ingredient in line drawings and illustrations (particularly of the technical, medical and biological kind). Indeed, Dwyer's research discussed earlier showed this to be true. In his 1978 text, Dwyer reviews his studies on the effectiveness of colour in illustrations and lists over 30 studies (in addition to his own) that show colour to be an effective instructional variable.

None the less, in view of the discussion below on learning to read illustrations, it might be expected that the conventions that we adults accept so naturally concerning the use of colour in illustrations have to be taught to children. In many situations the use of full colour is essential if learners are to make correct discriminations. The debate about whether or not to use colour, and if so how much colour to use, arises in situations when colour is not absolutely necessary. Particular difficulties can then arise with (i) using too many colours indiscriminately, and (ii) using too few colours (say only two) to denote more than two functions.

In a useful review of the functions of a second colour in printed text, Waller *et al.* (1982) point out that a second colour may be useful:

- where pointed lines linking labels to diagrams might be confusing if only one colour is used;
- where a coloured grid might be superimposed over a black and white illustration to indicate, for example, some sort of grouping; and
- where there might be two or more levels of text running in parallel (eg, study guidance being differentiated by colour from mainstream subject matter).

I would argue here that if only one or two extra colours are being used, then they must be used consistently and only when it seems necessary to make a point. There is no need to use colour on every page simply because it is technically possible to do so.

In specifying the use of colour printing it is useful to keep the following points in mind:

1. About 8.5 per cent of males and 0.5 per cent of females are colour-blind to some extent.
2. If reference is to be made by the author or the teacher to the function of the colour, then the colour must have a name in the language of the reader.
3. A pale colour, visible when seen as a large area, may be almost invisible when used to print a word or a fine line.
4. A dark colour will appear almost black when used to print a word or a fine line.
5. Bright colours set up a dazzle effect when printed as words or fine lines.
6. Black ink printed on white paper has the best contrast value.
7. Legibility is impaired when black text is printed on a strongly coloured ground.
8. Legibility is severely impaired when text is printed over a broken ground such as an illustration or a photograph.
9. Strong colour or a strong pattern in black and white or colour will be an irritant if it is positioned close to the text at the periphery of the visual field.
10. If the printed page is liable to be copied in black and white, using photographic or other means, then the coloured parts will appear as black or grey, or may disappear completely.

For all these reasons the designer will have to consider carefully the use of colour in printed text. Similar considerations, of course, also arise with electronic text (see Chapter 13).

Learning to read diagrams and illustrations

It is well known that learning to read print is a complex skill that is painstakingly acquired. It is perhaps not so obvious that the same thing applies to learning to read illustrations and other tabular and graphic materials.

In point of fact very little seems to be known about how children learn to interpret pictures and how they develop skills in this respect.
Some researchers, for instance, have suggested that it is not until about the ages of 6 to 8 that children can reliably compare two pictures or diagrams and judge whether they are identical in all respects.
Other workers have suggested that this occurs a little earlier, depending

upon the type of task the child is asked to do (see Murphy and Wood, 1981). Several studies have shown that children find pictures ambiguous, that they are unable to interpret action elements, and that changes in scale are confusing. Similar findings have also been reported in studies of how adults who are unable to read interpret pictures. The idea expressed earlier that pictures will help less-able readers has to be reconsidered. Some readers will have to be given considerable support to help them deal with diagrams and illustrations in instructional text.

Furthermore, what may be obvious for an expert, creating the illustration, may not be at all obvious to a novice learner. Novices may not only have to deal with unfamiliar subject matter but they may also be hampered by their lack of knowledge about how to read a diagram or illustration. Lowe (1993) points out that beginners find *changes* in the use of conventions in the graphics in a particular text especially confusing.

Authors, therefore, need to assess the value and the effectiveness of their illustrations and diagrams. This can be done, somewhat crudely, by asking potential readers either singly, or in small groups, to comment on, explain, or discuss the proposed illustrative material with the author present. Such informal feedback should not be discounted. It is probably more informative in the initial stages than carrying out elaborate field tests (see Chapter 14).

Lowe (1993) indicates that there are a number of levels at which authors can collect information for evaluating the way learners respond to illustrations and diagrams. For example one can use:

- diagrams/illustrations alone
- diagrams/illustrations in conjunction with their accompanying instructional material
- diagrams/illustrations in the context of their use.

Such evaluation needs to address a variety of questions. Lowe lists the following general questions:

- Does the learner consider the diagram to be helpful?
- Does the learner process the diagram sufficiently deeply overall?
- Does the learner understand and remember the material presented?
- Can the learner apply the material presented?

And then some more specific ones, such as:

- Are there particular aspects of the diagram that learners find distracting, annoying or confusing?
- Does the learner explore the information provided in the diagram in a productive fashion?
- Does the learner deal effectively with the various transformations that have been used in the diagram?
- Can the learner identify all the entities shown in the diagram and assign them an appropriate role in the diagram's explanation of the subject matter?

- Can the learner locate all the important relations that exist among the diagram's entities?
- Does the learner integrate material in the diagram effectively with its accompanying materials?
- Can the learner translate the relations which the diagram depicts in visuo-spatial terms into their intended real-life meanings?
- Can the learner go beyond the diagram and use it to deal successfully with the actual subject matter of the diagram?

Summary

1. Diagrams and illustrations serve a variety of overlapping functions in instructional text: they can aid motivation, attention, instruction and recall.
2. The research suggests that illustrations aid the recall of text that is illustrated, but that they do not help much the recall of related (but not illustrated) text.
3. The positioning and the labelling of diagrams and illustrations is important for drawing the reader's attention to particular points in the text.
4. Scanners and clip art may make it easier to provide illustrative materials, but care should be given to their purpose and presentation.
5. Step-by-step pictures and strip cartoons are popular for instructional purposes but their design aspects have not been adequately researched.
6. Additional colour in printing is often unnecessary and the indiscriminate use of colour can cause additional problems.
7. Children have to learn the conventions used in illustrations that adults take for granted, and authors especially need to assess the effectiveness of their illustrations in this regard.

References

Booher, H R (1975) 'Relative comprehensibility of pictorial information and printed words in proceduralized instructions', *Human Factors*, 17, 3, 266–77.

Curran, T E (1978) 'Quantification of technical manual graphic comprehensibility', Report TN-78-2, Navy Personnel Research & Development Center, San Diego, CA 92152.

Dwyer, F M (1972) *A Guide for Improving Visualized Instruction*, Learning Services, Box 784, State College, Pennsylvania, PA 16801.

Dwyer, F M (1976) *Strategies for Improving Visual Learning*, Learning Services, Box 784, State College, Pennsylvania, PA 16801.

Dwyer, F M (1987) *Enhancing Visualized Instruction – Recommendations for Practitioners*, Learning Services, Box 784, State College, Pennsylvania, PA 16801.

Jones, B F *et al.* (1984) 'Content driven comprehension, instruction and assessment: a model for army training literature', Technical Report, Alexandria, VA: Army Research Institute.

Levie, W H and Lentz, R (1982) 'Effects of text illustrations: a review of research', *Educational Communication & Technology Journal, 30*, 4, 195–232.

Lowe, R. (1993) *Successful Instructional Diagrams*, London: Kogan Page.

Misanchuk, E R (1992) *Preparing Instructional Text: Document design using desktop publishing*, Englewood Cliffs, NJ: Educational Technology Publications.

Morrell, R W and Park, D C (1993) 'The effects of age, illustrations and task variables on the performance of procedural assembly tasks', *Psychology and Aging, 8*, 3, 389–99.

Murphy, C M and Wood, D J (1981) 'Learning from pictures: the use of pictorial information by young children', *Journal of Experimental and Child Psychology, 32*, 279–97.

Szlichcinski, C (1984) 'Factors affecting the comprehension of pictographic instruction', in Easterby, R and Zwaga, H (eds) *Information Design*, Chichester: Wiley.

Twyman, M (1979) 'A schema for the study of graphic language', in Kolers, P A *et al.* (eds) *Processing of Visual Language, Vol. 1*, New York: Plenum.

Waller, R, Lefrere, P and Macdonald-Ross, M (1982) 'Do you need that second color?', *IEEE Transactions on Professional Communication, 25*, 2, 80–85.

Suggested further reading

Anglin, G J (1987) 'Effect of pictures on recall of written prose: how durable are picture effects?', *Educational Communication & Technology Journal, 35*, 25–30.

Briscoe, M H (1990) *A Researcher's Guide to Scientific and Medical Illustrations*, New York: Springer-Verlag.

Harnett, P (1993) 'Identifying progression in children's understanding: the use of visual materials to assess primary school children's learning in history', *Cambridge Journal of Education, 23*, 2, 137–54.

Harrison, R P (1981) *The Cartoon: Communication to the quick*, Beverly Hills: Sage.

Horton, W (1991) *Illustrating Computer Documentation*, New York: Wiley.

Houghton, H A and Willows, D M (eds) (1987) *The Psychology of Illustration, Vol.2*, New York: Springer-Verlag.

Howard, C W *et al.* (1991) 'The relative effectiveness of symbols and words to convey photocopier functions', *Applied Ergonomics, 22*, 4, 217–24.

Levin, J R and Mayer, R E (1993) 'Understanding illustrations in text', in Britton, B K, Woodward, A and Binkley, M (eds) *Learning from Textbooks*, Hillsdale, NJ: Erlbaum.

Mandl, H and Levin, J R (eds) (1989) *Knowledge Acquisition from Text and Pictures*, Amsterdam: North Holland.

Poggenpohl, J H and Winkler, D R (eds) (1992) 'Diagrams as tools for wordmaking', special issue of *Visible Language*, 26, 3 and 4, 250–473.

Sewell, E H and Moore, R L (1980) 'Cartoon embellishments in informative presentations', *Educational Communication & Technology Journal*, 28, 39–46.

Sless, D (1981) *Learning and Visual Communication*, London: Croom Helm.

Willows, D M and Houghton, H A (eds) (1987) *The Psychology of Illustration, Vol.1*, New York: Springer-Verlag.

Winn, W (1989) 'The design and use of instructional graphics', in Mandl, H and Levin, J R (eds) *Knowledge Acquisition from Text and Pictures*, Amsterdam: North Holland.

Zimmerman, M L and Perkin, G W (1982) 'Instructing people through pictures: print materials for people who do not read', *Information Design Journal*, 3, 2, 119–34.

9 Tables and graphs

▼

This chapter discusses issues to consider when displaying quantitative information. I suggest several guidelines and point out (1) that tables and graphs require as much care in their design and positioning as does the text itself, and (2) that children need to be taught the conventions used in displaying quantitative information.

▲

This chapter and the previous one consider some – but by no means all – of the ways of enhancing text. The topics considered in this chapter are tables and graphs.

Tables

Tables vary enormously in their complexity and detail. As Patricia Wright (1980) remarks,

> One of the striking similarities between prose and tables is the diversity of the materials to be found under each umbrella term. While prose varies from romantic short stories to lengthy physics textbooks, so tables vary from those which are entirely numerical (eg logarithmic tables) to those which are entirely verbal or use other symbolic notation (eg the periodic table of chemical elements).

According to Wright, three processes determine how easy it is for readers to use a table. These are:

1. *Comprehension processes* – do readers understand how the table has been organized?
2. *Search processes* – do readers know where to look to find the answers to their questions?
3. *Interpretative processes* – do readers know how to interpret the answers that they find in the table? Do the answers that they find provide all they need to know or do they need to compare these figures with other figures in the same, or other, tables?

The more complex the table, the more difficult is each of these three processes. Children in particular have trouble with complex tables and it is clear that we all have to acquire the conventions of reading and using graphic materials. In what ways might authors and designers simplify the task?

Simplifying the content

Ehrenberg (1977) argues that most statistical tables are badly presented and that their understanding requires a great deal of effort – even from sophisticated users. The criterion for a good table, according to Ehrenberg, is that patterns and exceptions should be obvious at a glance – at least once one knows what they are.

Ehrenberg provides four basic rules for presenting data in tables:

1. Drastically round off numbers so that readers can easily make meaningful comparison. (Compare Table 9/1a with Table 9/1b.)
2. Include averages. Averages not only summarize the data but they also allow one to grasp the spread between the above-average and the below-average values. (Compare Table 9/1b with Table 9/1c.)
3. Figures in columns are easier to compare than figures in rows. (Compare Table 9/1c with Table 9/1d.)
4. Order rows in columns by size. Larger numbers placed at the top help mental arithmetic. Ordering by size aids comparison. (This rule is more appropriate for single tables than it is for a series of tables

Table 9/1a

Thousands unemployed	1966	1968	1970	1973
Total	330.9	549.0	582.2	597.9
Males	259.6	450.7	495.3	499.4
Females	71.3	88.8	86.9	98.5

Table 9/1b

Thousands unemployed	1966	1968	1970	1973
Total	330	550	580	600
Males	260	460	500	500
Females	71	89	87	99

Table 9/1c

Thousands unemployed	1966	1968	1970	1973	Average
Total	330	550	580	600	520
Males	260	460	500	500	430
Females	71	89	87	99	86

Table 9/1d

	Unemployed (1000s)		
	Males	Females	Total
1973	500	99	600
1970	500	87	580
1968	460	89	550
1966	260	71	330
Average	430	86	520

where the order of sizes may vary; for a series of tables one must keep to the same overall structure throughout.)

Readers are referred to Ehrenberg's (1977) article for a fuller discussion of these guidelines.

Spacing the items

Simple tables, of the sort shown in Ehrenberg's examples, may suffer in clarity if they are presented in a balanced or justified form and if, in particular, they are spread or squeezed to match the width of the text. This can be particularly unfortunate if there are, say, only two columns in the table. Table 9/2a shows the traditional approach to table design. Table 9/2b shows the approach I would suggest. In Table 9/2b the eye movements between the columns in the table are small and regular – unlike those in Table 9/2a.

Table 9/2a

Place of meeting	%
School or college	34
Dance or dance hall	27
Private house	18
Work or forces	15
Street or public transport	10
Cafe or pub	6

Table 9/2b

%	Place of meeting
34	School or college
27	Dance or dance hall
18	Private house
15	Work or forces
10	Street or public transport
6	Cafe or pub

This argument can be taken further. If, in certain tables, some elements have consistent widths and some have variable ones, then it might be easier for the reader (as well as for the designer) to put all of the consistent items together. Table 9/3a shows an original format for a set of tables in a college prospectus. Table 9/3b shows a revision to this format: now the consistent items have been placed in sequence and the text is no longer set justified. This revision allowed all of the 200 or so tables in this prospectus to be spaced consistently. With the original layout each table had to be planned separately, and each looked different.

Table 9/3a

Class	Subject	Day	Time	Room
73005	Children's garments	Fri.	10–12	315
73015	Dress	Tues.	2–4	315
73105	Embroidery	Mon.	11/2–4	315
73135	Ladies' tailoring	Fri.	2–4	Ov15
73155	Soft furnishings	Tues.	10–12	315

Table 9/3b

Class	Day	Time	Room	Subject
73005	Fri.	10–12	315	Children's garments
73015	Tues.	2–4	315	Dress
73105	Mon.	11/2–4	315	Embroidery
73135	Fri.	2–4	Ov155	Ladies' tailoring
73155	Tues.	10–12	315	Soft furnishings

Finally, we might note that spacing may be used to group and separate items in tables, and thus to facilitate search and retrieval. If the columns are lengthy then regular line-spacing (about every five items) aids in this respect. In addition, extra headings may be useful for lengthy tables. Table 9/4a, for instance, was markedly improved in its effectiveness by making the simple alterations shown in Table 9/4b. Regular line-spacing was introduced between groups of items and extra side headings were provided. By changing the position of the entry 'London', people in the

Table 9/4a

	Rump steak	Pork chops	Potatoes	Butter	Margarine	Cheese
Athens	0.70 - 11	0.65 + 8	0.07 + 2	0.66 + 9	0.33 - 8	0.41 + 1
Bonn	1.35 - 11	0.97 + 3	0.03	0.71 + 2	0.37 + 4	1.05 + 32
Brussels	1.21 + 1	0.82 + 11	0.02	0.58 - 3	0.26 - 9	0.54 - 9
Copenhagen	1.47 + 14	0.33 + 6	0.07 + 3	0.67 + 13	0.27 - 4	0.75 + 14
Dublin	0.75 + 20	0.82 + 15	0.06 + 2	0.47 + 10	0.33 + 9	0.53 + 13
Geneva	2.30 + 9	1.30 - 3	0.09 + 2	0.70 + 2	0.45 - 7	0.98 + 4
Hague	1.07	0.76 + 1	0.06	0.57	0.16 - 1	0.72
London	1.34 + 33	0.72 + 3	0.04	0.31 + 7	0.29 + 5	0.42 + 2
Luxembourg	1.30 + 9	0.65 + 11	0.02	0.58 + 3	0.32 + 2	0.80
Oslo	0.94 - 68	1.12 + 7	0.07 - 1	0.42 + 2	0.21 - 8	0.59 + 14
Paris	1.32 + 25	0.83 + 15	0.04 - 2	0.71 + 9	0.29 + 1	0.55 + 25
Rome	1.21 + 10	0.85 + 8	0.04 - 1	0.85 + 12	0.15 + 5	0.76 + 3
Stockholm	1.28 + 6	0.91 + 2	0.08 + 1	0.56	0.35 - 15	0.74 + 4
Vienna	1.21 + 6	0.89 + 1	0.09 + 5	0.61 + 3	0.34 + 2	0.58 + 8

The plus/minus figures are changes in the past six months. Prices in £ per pound.

Table 9/4b

	Rump steak	Pork chops	Potatoes	Butter	Margarine	Cheese	
London	1.34 + 33	0.72 + 3	0.04	0.31 + 7	0.29 + 5	0.42 + 2	London
Athens	0.70 - 11	0.65 + 8	0.07 + 2	0.66 + 9	0.33 - 8	0.41 + 1	Athens
Bonn	1.35 - 11	0.97 + 3	0.03	0.71 + 2	0.37 + 4	1.05 + 32	Bonn
Brussels	1.21 + 1	0.82 + 11	0.02	0.58 - 3	0.26 - 9	0.54 - 9	Brussels
Copenhagen	1.47 + 14	0.33 + 6	0.07 + 3	0.67 + 13	0.27 - 4	0.75 + 14	Copenhagen
Dublin	0.75 + 20	0.82 + 15	0.06 + 2	0.47 + 10	0.33 + 9	0.53 + 13	Dublin
Geneva	2.30 + 9	1.30 - 3	0.09 + 2	0.70 + 2	0.45 - 7	0.98 + 4	Geneva
Hague	1.07	0.76 + 1	0.06	0.57	0.16 - 1	0.72	Hague
Luxembourg	1.30 + 9	0.65 + 11	0.02	0.58 + 3	0.32 + 2	0.80	Luxembourg
Oslo	0.94 - 68	1.12 + 7	0.07 - 1	0.42 + 2	0.21 - 8	0.59 + 14	Oslo
Paris	1.32 + 25	0.83 + 15	0.04 - 2	0.71 + 9	0.29 + 1	0.55 + 25	Paris
Rome	1.21 + 10	0.85 + 8	0.04 - 1	0.85 + 12	0.15 + 5	0.76 + 3	Rome
Stockholm	1.28 + 6	0.91 + 2	0.08 + 1	0.56	0.35 - 15	0.74 + 4	Stockholm
Vienna	1.21 + 6	0.89 + 1	0.09 + 5	0.61 + 3	0.34+ 2	0.58 + 8	Vienna

The plus/minus figures are changes in the past six months. Prices in £ per pound.

United Kingdom were able to compare much more easily the price of foods in other countries with those in London – the actual aim of the table.

The examples given here show that tables can be designed to present information clearly without the use of printers' lines or 'rules'. The use of horizontal rules can help to group information but it is best to avoid an excessive use of rules. Completely boxing in tables is not usually necessary and complicating the display in this way reduces clarity. If rules are to be used to group data it is best not to use more than two clearly differentiated thicknesses of line.

Organizing the content

The organization of the content of tables needs to reflect the reader's task in using the table. Often with simple materials (such as a calendar) it does not matter much if the days are listed vertically or horizontally. But, even here, if a designer takes an aesthetic rather than a functional approach, the results can be difficult to use. Try working out what the date will be three weeks on Saturday in Table 9/5, for example.

Table 9/5

A decorative approach to designing a calendar which makes it difficult to use.

JANUARY

FRI	SAT	SUN	MON	TUE	WED	THU	FRI	SAT	SUN	MON	TUE	WED	THU	FRI	SAT	SUN	MON	TUE	WED
1	2	3	4	5	6	7	8	9	10	11	12	13	14	15	16	17	18	19	20

THU	FRI	SAT	SUN	MON	TUE	WED	THU	FRI	SAT	SUN
21	22	23	24	25	26	27	28	29	30	31

FEBRUARY

MON	TUE	WED	THU	FRI	SAT	SUN	MON	TUE	WED	THU	FRI	SAT	SUN	MON	TUE	WED	THU	FRI	SAT
1	2	3	4	5	6	7	8	9	10	11	12	13	14	15	16	17	18	19	20

SUN	MON	TUE	WED	THU	FRI	SAT	SUN
21	22	23	24	25	26	27	28

MARCH

MON	TUE	WED	THU	FRI	SAT	SUN	MON	TUE	WED	THU	FRI	SAT	SUN	MON	TUE	WED	THU	FRI	SAT
1	2	3	4	5	6	7	8	9	10	11	12	13	14	15	16	17	18	19	20

SUN	MON	TUE	WED	THU	FRI	SAT	SUN	MON	TUE	WED
21	22	23	24	25	26	27	28	29	30	31

Ehrenberg, as we have noted above, suggests that columns of figures should be organized vertically. Table 9/1c might be clearer if it presented the totals beneath the entries for the males and females because this would match our normal expectations that such numbers would be summed. Bartram (1984), however, has suggested that bus timetables are better understood when the route listings are placed horizontally across the top of the timetable than when they are placed vertically. He feels that this more clearly reflects the notion of a journey going in a particular direction. So rows and columns have to ordered in a way that makes intuitive sense.

Of course deliberations such as these do not take into account printing practice. Tables are usually designed to fit particular column widths.

Thus tables are sometimes re-oriented to make them fit without considering the needs of the reader. In point of fact, it would be difficult to re-orient Tables 9/4a and 9/4b for instance, because there are more town entries than there are food entries. However, this difficulty could be overcome by printing the names of the towns vertically – but this is not a recommended practice. Finally, in print, it may be possible to present tables sideways on the page, but this option is not available in electronic text (see Norrish, 1984).

Once again, may I reiterate in this section that if several tables of the same kind are to be presented then it should go without saying that it is appropriate to keep these tables in the same format throughout the text. In an article I once read, there were five simple tables. The first four of these were in the format:

	1	2
A	—	—
B	—	—

but the last one, for some reason was presented thus:

	A	B
1	—	—
2	—	—

This led me to misread it. It is important, when reviewing one's text, to check for simple issues such as this.

Guidelines

Some specific guidelines for constructing tables are as follows:

- Make a rough draft first in planning tables. A square grid underlay will be especially helpful. Start from the left.
- Use space systematically and consistently to indicate which blocks of material go together.
- If the table is wide and contains many columns, then row headings can be placed both to the left and the right to help comprehension (see Table 9/4b).
- If the columns are lengthy, use regular line-spacing (about every five items), as this helps retrieval (see Table 9/4b).
- If there are many rows and columns, then space can be saved by numbering or lettering them. However, it is best, if at all possible, to avoid the use of numerous columns and rows and consequent footnotes.
- Avoid excessive typographic cueing.
- If the table captions are numbered use Arabic rather than Roman numerals.

- Write a clear but informative caption: tell the reader what the table shows.
- Test out tables with appropriate learners to see what happens when they are asked to use them. Lowe's (1993) guidelines, given in Chapter 8, are also applicable here.

New technology and table design

It may appear, on the face of it, that tables have a number of basic structures that can be classified and coded to produce templates for electronic processing. Unfortunately, people who have attempted to create taxonomies of table-types have not found the matter to be so simple. None the less, this has not prevented people from trying.

The report by Paul Lefrere (1989) provides an illuminating illustration of the difficulties and the possibilities in this area. This report presents an account and assessment of research carried out at the Open University into the feasibility of writing computer programs to help with tabular composition and editing. A prototype program developed for the Apple Macintosh allowed users to create and manipulate tables in a structural way, and to see the results on screen. Lefrere reports that the time taken to construct tables was markedly reduced and illustrations are provided of how tables were improved (along the lines argued in this text) with the use of the program.

Graphs

In 1979 the US National Institute of Education issued a request for a proposal for research into the presentation and comprehension of graphical displays. The introduction to the proposal made the following observations:

> These visual displays of information are an important means of communication and have become tools for thinking in all scientific and technical fields. . . . Recent technological advances in computer graphics suggest that both students and ordinary citizens will be confronted with increasing demands on their ability to comprehend information from graphs and charts. . . . Unfortunately, the technological advances in producing graphs and charts have not been accompanied by any significant amount of research about people's comprehension of the displays which are produced.

Most of the research available on how children and adults understand graphs has used simple print presentations and it has not involved work with graphs on screens, although there have been developments in this direction. Furthermore, most of this research is of the comparison kind. For example, a typical question might be: 'Is a line graph better than a bar chart?' Such a question is oversimple: the answer depends upon a number of factors, including the requirements of the reader. The findings from research of this kind are complex and need teasing out carefully. The papers by Macdonald-Ross (1977, a and b) and the text by Tufte (1983) are essential reading for anyone undertaking research in this area. I have drawn some (probably oversimple) conclusions from this research in the next few paragraphs. These issues are important to consider now that computer programs enable the same set of data to be presented in a variety of different ways at the touch of a button.

It is often thought that the simplest kinds of graph, and the easiest to understand, are line graphs and bar charts. This assumption may be true, but it depends upon the type of information being sought. Generally speaking, line graphs are probably better than bar charts or tables for showing trends, and tables are probably better than line graphs for showing exact quantities. But a lot depends upon the data. Consider for example Table 9/6 and Figures 9/1a, 9/1b and 9/1c. Here the same data have been presented in different ways using the Harvard Graphics program. In this example, Table 9/6 shows the trend for murders rather better than Figures 9/1a, 9/1b or 9/1c.

Table 9/6

Approximate number of offences recorded by policemen in England and Wales, 1950–1990.

	1950	1960	1970	1980	1990
Robberies	1000	2000	6300	15000	36000
Rapes	200	500	900	1200	3400
Murders	300	400	400	600	700

Pie charts are said to be easy to understand, but they may also be misleading. It is difficult to judge the proportions accurately when the segments are small (see Figure 9/2). It is also difficult to put the lettering in clearly. Pie charts give a general impression of quantitative relationships but, compared with bar charts, subtle differences are more difficult to detect. Quantitative differences are more readily discernible in bar charts because they are based on multiples of a square module or a regular unit of two-dimensional space.

Pie charts are also difficult to understand if charts with different diameters are being compared. One possible reason for this is that in order to make a circle (or a square) look twice as large, the large one has to be drawn almost four times the size of the small one.

For the same general reason, when the task of the reader is to estimate percentages and quantities, bar charts are better methods of presentation than are cross-sections of three-dimensional objects, such as spheres, cubes and blocks of columns.

Figure 9/1a

A line graph to show the same data as Table 9/6.

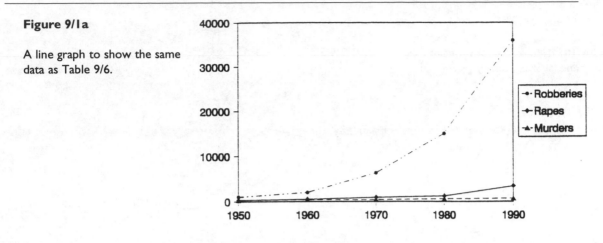

Figure 9/1b

A bar chart to show the same data.

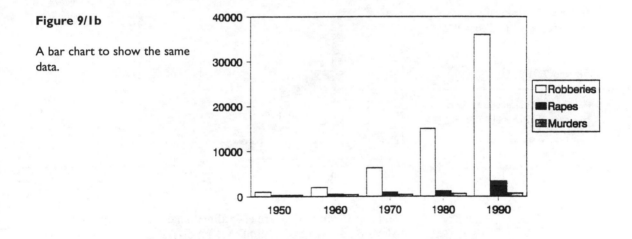

Figure 9/1c

A compound bar chart to show the same data.

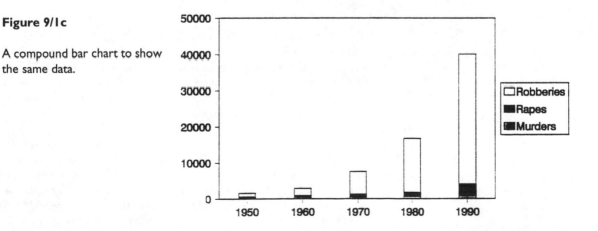

Figure 9/2

The difficulties of both seeing and labelling small segments on pie-charts.

Figure 9/3a

A three-dimensional display of the data shown in Figure 9/2.

Figure 9/3b

A two-dimensional display of the data shown in Figure 9/2

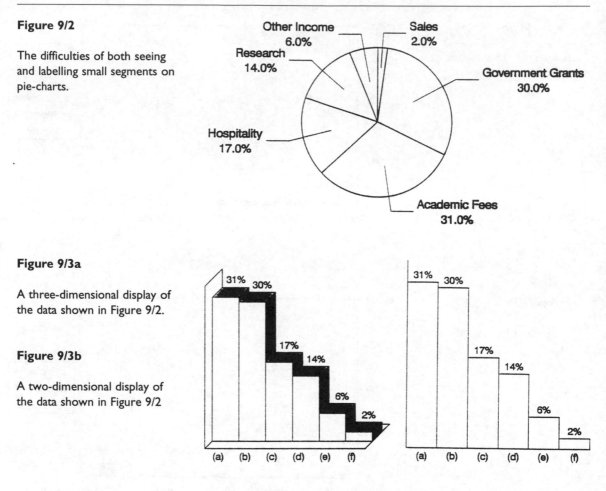

Today it is common to see such three-dimensional graphs on our television screens and in published reports. Figure 9/3a shows a typical example. Experience and research would suggest that two-dimensional displays are easier to understand than three-dimensional ones (see Figure 9/3b).

Typographic cueing is often used to excess in graphical displays. The message here is, as before, to keep things simple. Misanchuk (1992) suggests that bar charts may look more pleasing if, rather than mixing a variety of patterns, shades of grey are used in an ordered progression. Personally, I would not even have different shades of grey, as such subtleties are often lost when the material is copied.

The aim of a graph is to communicate findings easily and clearly. As the vertical and horizontal scales on graphs can be stretched or compressed in order to make points more forcefully, learners need to be made aware of such strategies. Figure 9/4 shows that when the same data are plotted with different vertical axes, different impressions are conveyed. Tufte (1983) devotes two chapters to discussing what he calls 'graphical integrity'.

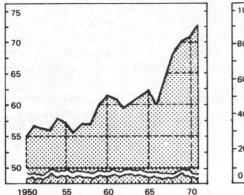 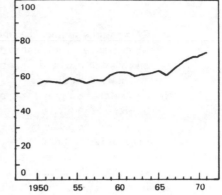

Figure 9/4

What happens when
the same data are
plotted with different
vertical axes.

The authors of instructional materials are not necessarily the best
people to create graphical aids. Features such as these require a
knowledge of and a respect for standardized signs and drawing
conventions, as well as a knowledge of legibility features.

Transfer lettering is frequently used in the preparation of artwork for
instructional text. Although apparently easy to apply, great care needs
to be used to ensure the proper spacing of character groups. Figure 9/5
shows how the unskilled use of transfer lettering can lead to poor quality
labelling. Transfer lettering is useful but it is more difficult to use than is
sometimes supposed. Certainly, no one without a knowledge of lettering
or of legibility requirements should use it for making headings and
labels. It is far better to tell professionals what is required, and to have
them provide examples.

Figure 9/5

Transfer lettering requires
great care with alignment and
spacing.

educational

educational

The labelling of graphs should not confuse the reader, either through its
positioning or by the careless placing of lines which connect the label to
its referent. Indeed, in designing instructional text, graphical aids to
comprehension need as much care and thought in their making and
positioning as do other parts of the text.

Other factors which limit the legibility of graphical aids are:

1. Words set at an angle from the horizontal.
2. Reversed lettering, that is, white characters on a black or a strong or
    dark-coloured background.
3. Show-through, that is, the appearance on the page of the lines or
    drawings printed on the reverse side.

Guidelines

- Keep graphs simple. Use line graphs or bar charts where possible.
- Make a rough draft first to get the sizes in proportion and to see how much space you need. Do not cram graphs in. Use an underlying grid and start from the left.
- If the aim of the graph is to compare different conditions then several lines can be plotted on the same graph. However, if more than two or three lines are presented this can be confusing, and it is probably best to separate the lines by typographic cues (eg, different symbols or colours) or to use separate graphs. If possible, label the lines on a line graph directly, rather than use a key.
- If space permits, letter horizontally both the vertical and the horizontal axes. It is sometimes helpful to put actual numbers on the sides of the bars in a vertical bar chart or on the top of them in a horizontal one.
- Avoid footnotes if possible.
- Write a clear but informative caption: tell the reader what the graph shows.
- Test out the graph with appropriate learners to see what happens when they are asked to use it. Again, Lowe's (1993) guidelines, given in Chapter 8, are applicable here.

Positioning tables and graphs in the text

Tables, graphs and other illustrative materials do not appear on their own: they fit into a context. Such devices are embedded in a textual argument, and authors use devices like 'See Figure 3' or 'Figure 3 shows that...' to draw the readers' attention to a figure and to what it is that they are supposed to see.

Thus, the positioning of tables, graphs and other illustrative materials in the text deserves more careful consideration than it often appears to receive. In scientific articles, and in textbooks too, it is not unusual to find such materials divorced from their textual references. This happens because of the standard practice of positioning such material at the top or bottom of a column of print. Clearly it is not always possible to put tables and illustrative materials in their appropriate places, especially when there are runs of several tables, large tables, and page turn-over decisions to be made. (This chapter provides a good example of such complexities.) However, with the advent of desk-top publishing it should be much easier to place these materials close to where they are first mentioned in the text.

Tables and graphs are usually (but not always) given captions, but these captions are often limited. Captions usually describe but they do not often explain. Thus a caption which says 'Table 3: the results of Experiment 1' does not communicate what conclusions can be drawn from the table. A more instructive caption might read something like, 'Table 3 shows how the experimental group outperformed the control group on every measure except...'.

Concluding comments

In 1988 the UK Department of Education and Science's Assessment and Performance Unit reported on the ability of 11- and 15-year-old children to read and to use tables and graphs. Children aged 11 were asked to read from, to add data to, and to construct tables, pie charts, bar charts and line graphs. Children aged 15 completed similar tasks, together with a number of other more complicated tasks, such as reading cross-sectional diagrams. Table 9/7 shows the overall performance for the 11-year-olds on the main tasks. The results were similar for the 15-year-olds. The authors of the report indicated that the majority of children could do simple tasks and answer simple questions with these materials, but that their performance fell markedly when the questions got more difficult. This was particularly the case for the average and the less-able children.

Table 9/7

Shows the average performance of 11-year-olds on tests of their ability to read, to add to, and to create graphical materials (source DES, 1988a).

Questions on:	Number of test questions	Overall average score (%)	Range of scores (%)
tables	32	68	41–92
pie charts	25	65	33–93
bar charts	40	61	18–89
graphs	53	55	21–81

Macdonald-Ross (1977b) concluded his review of the presentation of quantitative data as follows:

> No one graphic format is universally superior to all others, though some are so unsatisfactory that they can be virtually discarded from the armoury. To choose the best format for a particular occasion one must decide: What kind of data is to be shown? What teaching points need to be made? What will the learner do with the data? Can previous models be copied? Do we have the time and the skills to execute the format? ... It pays to remember that graphic communication is an *art*, that is, a skill which results from knowledge and practice.

It is obviously pointless to expect children to understand and create tables and graphs automatically. Unless the skills are taught, as reading and writing are taught, such aids will have little value in instructional materials.

Summary

1. Tables and graphs benefit from being kept simple. The typography of such materials should have a high standard of legibility. Poorly designed materials (in terms of internal logic as well as presentation) present extra difficulties.
2. Searching, interpreting, and understanding is facilitated by the careful use of spacing, and the removal of clutter.
3. The positioning of tables and graphs requires careful planning. Such materials should not be positioned on a page irrespective of their textual reference, or placed on a 'let's put this here' basis to fill up a vacant space.
4. The more complex these materials are, the greater the difficulties for less-able readers.
5. Different formats have different purposes. In choosing an appropriate format one needs to consider: Who are the likely readers? What skills will they have? What teaching points need to be made? What are the readers required to do with the data?

References

Bartram, D (1984) 'The presentation of information about bus services', in Easterby, R and Zwaga, H (eds) *Information Design*, Chichester: Wiley.

DES (1988a) *Science at Age 11: A review of APU findings 1980–1984*, London: HMSO.

DES (1988b) *Science at Age 15: A review of APU findings 1980–1984*, London: HMSO.

Ehrenberg, A S C (1977) 'Rudiments of numeracy', *Journal of the Royal Statistical Society A*, 140, 227–97.

Lefrere, P (1989) 'Design aids for constructing and editing tables', *British Library Research Paper*, 61, London: British Library.

Lowe, R (1993) *Successful Instructional Diagrams*, London: Kogan Page.

Macdonald-Ross, M (1977a) 'Graphics in text', in Shulman, L S (ed.) *Review of Research in Education Vol 5*, Ithaca, Ill: Peacock.

Macdonald-Ross, M (1977b) 'How numbers are shown: a review of research on the presentation of quantitative data in texts', *Audio Visual Communication Review*, 25, 359–409.

Misanchuk, E R (1992) *Preparing Instructional Text: Document design using desktop publishing*, Englewood Cliffs, NJ: Educational Technology Publications.

Norrish, P (1984) 'Moving tables from paper to screen', *Visible Language, XVIII*, 154–70.

Tufte, E R (1983) *The Visual Display of Quantitative Information*, Graphics Press, Box 430, Cheshire, CT 06410.

Wright, P (1980) 'The comprehension of tabulated information. Some similarities between reading prose and reading tables', *NSPI Journal, XIX*, 8, 25–9.

Suggested further reading

Beattie, V and Jones, M J (1992) *The Communication of Information Using Signs in Corporate Annual Reports*, London: The Chartered Association of Certified Accountants.

Bernard, M (1990) 'Using extended captions to improve learning from instructional illustrations', *British Journal of Educational Technology*, 21, 215–25.

Black, A and Rayner, M (1992) *Just Read the Label: Understanding nutrition information in numeric, verbal and graphic formats*, The Coronary Prevention Group, London: HMSO.

Boehm-Davis, D A *et al.* (1989) 'Effects of different data base formats on information retrieval', *Human Factors*, 31, 5, 579–72.

Briscoe, M H (1990) *A Researcher's Guide to Scientific and Medical Illustrations*, New York: Brock/Springer.

Constable, H, Campbell, B and Brown, R (1988) 'Sectional drawings from science textbooks: an experimental investigation into pupils' understanding', *British Journal of Educational Psychology*, 58, 89–102.

Hartley, J (1991) 'Tabling information', *American Psychologist*, 46, 6, 655–56.

Newton, D P (1993) 'Learning from tables', *Educational Psychology*, 13, 2, 89–103.

Swatton, P and Taylor, R M (1994) 'Pupil performance in graphical tasks and its relationship to the ability to handle variables', *British Educational Research Journal*, 20, 2, 227–43.

Technical Reports from the Advisory Group on Computer Graphics, Computer Centre, Loughborough University, Loughborough LE11 3TU.

Tufte, E R (1990) *Envisioning Information*, Graphics Press, PO Box 430, Cheshire, CT 06410.

Spence, D and Lewandowsky, J (1991) 'Display proportions and percentages', *Applied Cognitive Psychology*, 5, 61–77.

Wainer, H (1992) 'Understanding graphs and tables', *Educational Researcher*, 21, 1, 12–23.

10 Forms and questionnaires

This chapter discusses the layout and content of forms and questionnaires. I draw attention to the costs of completing and processing badly designed materials, and to the need for initial testing in order to eliminate obvious difficulties. I also consider the impact of new technology on the design of forms and questionnaires.

The layout of forms and questionnaires often presents considerable difficulties for the designer. Three aspects that need particularly to be borne in mind are:

1. Who is the form or questionnaire for?
2. How is it to be administered?
3. How are the data obtained to be processed?

These three facets of design can sometimes interact to their mutual disadvantage.

The costs of forms

In attempting to estimate the cost of forms and questionnaires, researchers have distinguished between the costs of *processing* these materials and the costs of *producing* them. Most investigators consider that the main costs lie in the processing of the data obtained. Indeed, it has been suggested that the cost of processing forms exceeds the cost of producing forms by a factor of 2 or 3. One extreme example quoted in the 1981 Rayner review of UK government forms illustrated the difference between processing and production costs: in this case it was estimated that one particular form cost 3p to print and £4 to process.

One additional figure which is not so easy to assess is the costs to the respondent of badly designed forms and questionnaires. Poorly designed materials can take a long time to complete and they can lead to errors and mistakes. Such errors on forms can result in respondents failing to obtain certain benefits or even – in extreme cases – being prosecuted for giving false information. Errors made on forms usually lead to greater processing time and forms may have to be returned to the respondents for correction, thus starting the cycle again.

Designing forms and questionnaires

The design principles advocated in the early chapters of this book also apply to the design of forms and questionnaires. However, these materials are often more difficult to design because of their complexity. Waller (1984) lists, for instance, the following typical items on a government form:

- form title
- form code number
- initial instructions
- part headings
- 'write clearly' and similar reminders
- primary questions
- supplementary questions
- question qualifiers/explanations
- tick boxes and their labels
- response space labels
- special notes next to response spaces to deal with typical errors predicted by pre-testing
- conditional user directions ('if you ticked yes ...')
- 'for office use' area
- page-break guides ('[section name] continued', 'Now please turn the page', etc.)
- declaration.

It is clear that systematic spacing in the text is required to help the respondent to deal with such complexity. A basic grid, as an underlying guide to organization, is essential. Standard paper sizes (particularly A4) should be considered, as such pages will fit into the standard envelope styles which are post office preferred. (The minimum size of these envelopes is 90 mm × 140 mm, the maximum 120 mm × 235 mm.)

It is generally accepted that forms and questionnaires that are clearly laid out are more likely to be returned than those which are not. However, it is also a common experience when filling in a form to find that space has been sacrificed in order to save on paper costs. If people anticipate that a form is going to be difficult to fill in, then this may lead to procrastination or the form not being completed at all. One research study showed how two factors, attractiveness and length, could interact. The authors reduced a 21-page questionnaire to three pages by using a matrix rather than a list format (see below). However, the three-page matrix format looked more difficult and this led to significantly fewer questionnaires being returned.

For my own personal amusement I have kept copies of badly designed forms and questionnaires that I have received and filled in over the years. An analysis of the errors that I have made suggests that the common faults in these forms are:

- insufficient space for my name;
- insufficient space for my address;
- inappropriate sequencing, leading me to respond in the wrong place;
- oddly positioned instructions – once the last instruction on a form that I had already filled in asked me (too late) to complete it in capital letters;
- instructions in type so small that I need a magnifying glass;

- strings of instructions in capital letters;
- multiple cueing – words in bold, capitals, italic, and different sizes all on the same form;
- abbreviations which I cannot follow;
- complex, lengthy and sometimes confusing questions.

I would have thought that most of these design errors are obvious, but clearly they are not – until they are pointed out. The designers of forms and questionnaires need to work through a checklist of some kind (perhaps based on the list above) before using their materials in an initial try-out. Undoubtedly such a procedure would have prevented the errors made in the form shown in Figure 10/1.

Figure 10/1

A typical form – with insufficient space for an address.

Publication Order

Payment required with order unless you have made prior arrangement with us. Discounts available for Members and Subscribers of the Institute, resellers, and bulk orders.

Name of the publication you are ordering
Annual Report

Name of your organisation
University of Keele

No. of copies
1

Payment Enclosed
$ 70.00

Your name and position
J. Hartley. Head

Your telephone number and extension

Delivery address
Dept. Psychology
University of Keele, Staffs

If you would like to be placed on our mailing list please tick this box ✔

ST5. 5BG. UK

The language of forms and questionnaires

The general points made in Chapter 6 about writing instructional text apply to the writing of forms and questionnaires – only more so. The main difficulty, commented on by many researchers, is that designers do not seem to consider the language, the logic and the layout of these materials from the respondent's perspective. If the sequence of questions is constrained by the needs of an administrator then the logic of a form or questionnaire may seem unnatural to the respondent. The respondent's expectations of what they will be asked next may make them misread subsequent questions, or lead them to give additional information which is irrelevant or out of context.

The need for precision in forms and questionnaires can present especial difficulties. Examples of gobbledegook abound, and there is no need to repeat them here. We all know from everyday experience the difficulties that confront us in understanding government forms, but perhaps the greatest difficulties are faced by the less-able and by those with limited language ability. Consider, for example, this piece of text from a form provided by the US Immigration and Naturalization Service:

> If you are the spouse or unmarried minor child of a person who has been granted preference classification by the Immigration and Naturalization Service or has applied for preference classification,

and you are claiming the same preference classification, or if you are claiming special immigrant classification as the spouse or unmarried child of a minister of religion who has been accorded or is seeking classification as a special immigrant, submit the following. . . .

One way of helping forms and questionnaire designers to overcome such problems has been to provide them with a thesaurus of alternative expressions which are more easily understood than are the expressions typically used by government officials. The British Department of Health and Social Security's (1983) *Good Forms Guide* contained such a thesaurus, and a much abbreviated version of this is provided in an appendix to this chapter. Today, of course, many computer-aided writing programs provide this kind of assistance at the touch of a button.

Asking questions

One special difficulty with the language of forms and questionnaires lies in the variety of ways in which questions can be asked and in which answers can be given. Common deficiencies include questions which:

- are ambiguous;
- are unintelligible;
- ask too much at once;
- limit the respondents' ability to provide the required information (by providing too narrow a range of response options and/or too little space for answers);
- ask for information of a kind that may be provided more readily in some other way;
- yield answers that cannot be easily processed;
- provide unwanted information.

Figure 10/2 shows the mess that can ensue when a variety of methods of questioning and answering are used on a single form. Figure 10/2 shows *six* different methods being used. Research has not fully established whether or not any one particular method is preferable to another – they all have advantages and limitations, as we shall see. However, from the point of view of consistency and ease of completion, it might be helpful if designers could keep to one or two methods of questioning within a single form or questionnaire.

- *Character separators*

  1. Studies have shown that writing one letter per box in a framework such as framework 2 takes respondents more time and the result is less legible than writing in

  2.

  3.

  4.

  frameworks 3 and 4. Framework 1, surprisingly, produces the worst results and framework 4 the best. Typing answers in constrained boxes can also cause difficulties.

- *Unconstrained answers*

  Often insufficient space is left for unconstrained answers. If your name was Fred Smith you could just fit it in this amount of space

  What would you do, however, if your name was

Figure 10/2

This form asks the reader to respond in six different ways. (Figure reproduced with permission from Patricia Wright.)

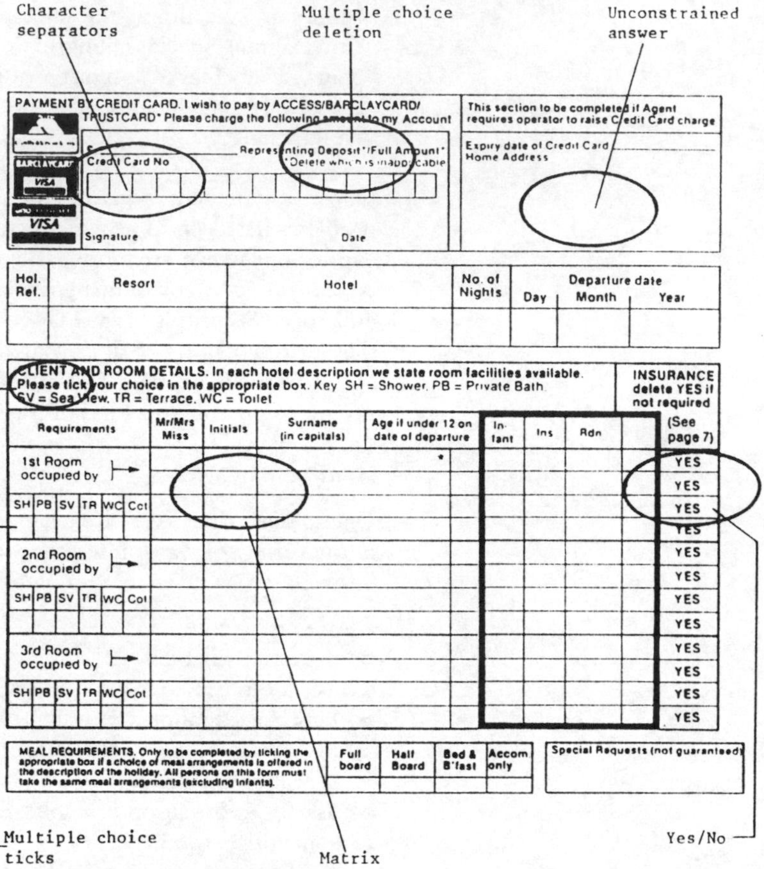

Madeleine Woodward-Waters? Answer spaces need to be big enough to fit the answer in, and they need to be located alongside the question being asked so that respondents know just where they are supposed to write. One should avoid the tendency (which often arises with justified composition) of having the answer space a long way from the end of the question.

- *Yes/no answers*
  This form of answer is perhaps the most simple, but this simplicity is perhaps deceptive. Respondents find it easier to answer questions that lead to the answer 'yes' rather than to the answer 'no'. Furthermore, questions demanding yes/no answers are often ambiguous, especially when there are two or more related parts. Patricia Wright provides the example of the question, 'Are you over 21 and under 65?' which gave particular difficulties to senior citizens who answered each part in turn.

- *Multiple-choice questions*
  With multiple-choice questions respondents have to indicate which choice is most appropriate for them. This can be achieved by a variety of methods, none of which is entirely satisfactory. Deletions can cause difficulties especially when negatives are concerned (eg, 'Delete what does *not* apply'). Ticking a particular choice usually

causes less difficulty, especially when positive responses are appropriate (eg, 'Tick which applies to you'). However, many people use ☑ or ☒ interchangeably and it is not clear whether ☒ means 'no' or 'yes'. Multiple-choice formats can cause additional difficulties when two or more pieces of information have to be combined in order to answer a question in a matrix format.

● *Matrix formats*
In matrix formats the reader has to refer to information presented in both the columns and the rows, and this can impose memory problems. These problems are increased when the number of rows and columns is more than three and when the respondents have to use coded letters to indicate their reply (eg, 'Give name of school if attending. Write D if dependant (see note D), P if of personable age (see note E), SB if receiving supplementary benefit'). Studies indicate that matrix formats can be redesigned in ways that markedly reduce memory loads, thus improving their effectiveness.

It is curious how many things can be ambiguous. In a previous form used by job applicants to Keele University, for example, the respondent was asked at one point: 'Give previous experience with dates'. One candidate for a lecturer's post replied, 'Moderately successful in the past, but I am now happily married!' In this example all that was required to remove the ambiguity was an additional comma: 'Give previous experience, with dates'. Factors such as these suggest the need for careful pre-testing of individual questions (and indeed whole forms and questionnaires) with small groups of appropriate respondents in order to eliminate such difficulties.

Sequencing information

The problems posed by asking questions are multiplied when such materials present different kinds of questions, as we saw in Figure 10/2. Furthermore, there is sometimes a problem with sequencing: questions may be asked in sequence; questions may be omitted; and questions may lead to different outcomes or branches. Patricia Wright (1981) suggests that three problems of sequencing are:

● *Linguistic* – questions and instructions must be clearly understood.
● *Logical* – branches must be organized to achieve the most economical flow.
● *Graphic* – the designer must display the pathway through the materials clearly so that all the irrelevant questions are skipped and all the relevant ones answered.

Adjunct materials

In addition to the main content of forms and questionnaires, there is the adjunct material – the instructions, the footnotes, the guides to completion, and 'the small print'.

An excess of instruction on how to complete a particular form or questionnaire can be confusing, especially if this is printed in small type. Indeed, many readers just ignore it. It may be better, therefore, to refer the reader – where appropriate – to separate notes (as with the current UK income tax form). This does not mean, of course, that the notes should be printed in small type, or in government jargon! Another useful alternative is to use a wide left-hand margin, and to place notes here, next to the item to be completed.

The initial instructions on how to complete a form or questionnaire can make great demands on the memory processes of form-fillers. Expecting respondents to remember the minutiae of such instructions is over-optimistic. No doubt reminders can be placed strategically throughout the materials but, of course, the better text the less that is required in the way of explanation of how it is to be completed.

Colour in forms and questionnaires

Many people enquire about what research has to say about the use of colour in forms. As noted in Chapter 8, colour can have at least two functions: it can be motivational and it can be functional. In terms of motivation, people often enquire about the use of different coloured papers and inks. I know of no research on the topic, but it may well be, for example, that a form printed on pink paper may seem less officious, or less off-putting than one on white paper. What little research there is – in the context of marketing – seems to have little positive to say about the effects of different coloured paper on return rates for mailed questionnaires and forms (Jobber and Sanderson, 1983).

In terms of functional requirements it might be helpful to have, say, all the answer-boxes in white, while the rest of the paper is, say, pale green. Such devices would indicate where responses are required. However, as suggested throughout this book, excessive amounts (and varied) colours should be avoided. Initial trials with small groups of potential respondents would no doubt prove useful in this respect.

The effects of new technology

Appearance and layout

One of the most dramatic effects of new technology on the design of forms and questionnaires has been on their appearance. Many authors of such materials readily use the facilities of desk-top publishing systems without paying careful attention to their effects. Many present-day forms and questionnaires seem to use multiple type-faces and type-sizes, boxes and rules, and clip art 'motivators' without considering how the readers may react.

Indeed I have such a questionnaire in front of me as I write this chapter. The text is clearly computer-based and to my mind full of problems. First of all the top and the bottom of the information areas are heavily ruled, creating a rigid framework. Then each question in the questionnaire is placed in a separately lightly ruled box. The width of each box is predetermined (there is a two-column structure), but the depth varies according to the amount of information per item. The information is forced to fit this width (with justified text) but if there is a lot of it, the type-size is reduced to help squeeze it in. Finally, there are also boxed instructional notes, commentaries and directions: these items are printed on a grey tinted background in different type-sizes, sometimes but not always in capital letters.

The authors of this questionnaire have requested that I do not display it here. They claim that it is a draft version, sent for my comments. They point out that the redeeming feature of desk-top publishing systems is that it is easy to change and modify the presentation as one goes along. This may be true, but I would want to start by arguing for consistency from the beginning, before trying it out on readers. None the less, trying out this questionnaire with appropriate respondents and critical judges (such as myself) did lead to improvements, both in the sequence and wording of the questions, and in its overall appearance.

Computer-aided forms design

It is anticipated that computer programs will be (and in fact have been) developed to help designers create forms and questionnaires. Templates may be used to ensure consistency but one critic has remarked that many of the products of these programs (in the mid-1980s) 'appear to have been designed as if humans didn't exist'.

Processing forms and questionnaires

The requirements of automatic data-processing have also had a marked effect on the design of forms and questionnaires, but probably not for the better as far as users are concerned. The development of optical scanners has led to a significant increase in the use of formats which employ multiple-choice rather than open-ended questions. Furthermore, in order to speed up data-processing, coded answers often have to be entered on to another separate sheet. Sometimes, for example, each of the multiple-choice alternatives is given a number and questions are answered by writing down the numbers chosen on a separate response sheet. In even more complicated situations more than one answer may be permitted, the possible combinations are all given numbers, and it is the choice of one of these numbers that has to be recorded elsewhere. (Such a system has been used by several examining boards in the UK.) The result of all this seems to be unnecessarily complicated for the user. Indeed there is evidence that shows that such complex response requirements can lead to an increase in errors.

Interactive forms

One advance we may now expect is the development of interactive forms and questionnaires displayed on visual display units (VDUs). This particular advance is to be welcomed because it will allow questions to be posed one at a time or in related groups, and the sequencing of the questions to depend upon the responses given to each item (see Gilbert, 1991). Such automated sequencing will thus remove one of the major problems of form design. In addition, answer-spaces need not be constrained in electronic forms: the next question may be presented when the reader completes the current one. Undoubtedly, computer-assisted form-filling will present additional problems – users will have to be able to operate computer terminals. Also some traditional problems – how to phrase the questions and how to present them clearly – will still remain.

▼

Summary

1. Poorly designed forms and questionnaires are costly for users and costly for their originators. They take longer to fill in, they produce more errors and they take longer to process.
2. An attractive layout is likely to help response rates: forms and questionnaires that look difficult to complete may lead to procrastination or no response at all.
3. The style and wording of forms and questionnaires needs to be simple, clear and appropriate to the user.
4. The ways of writing questions and the ways of asking for responses are many and varied. It would seem helpful to try to limit materials in this respect.
5. New technology has led to forms and questionnaires which are badly designed and difficult to complete. Interactive computer-assisted form-filling, however, offers useful advantages.

▲

References

Gilbert, N (1991) 'Support for members of the public', in Bench-Capon, T (ed.) *Knowledge-based Systems and Legal Applications*, London: Academic Press.

Jobber, D and Sanderson, S (1983) 'The effects of a prior letter and coloured questionnaire paper on mail survey response rates', *Journal of the Market Research Society*, 25, 3, 339–49.

Waller, R (1984) 'Designing a government form: a case history', *Information Design Journal*, 4, 36–57.

Wright, P (1981) 'Informed design for forms', *Information Design Journal*, 2, 2, 151–8.

Suggested further reading

Brockman, R J (1993) 'Review of FormsDesigner', *Information Design Journal*, 7, 2, 171–74.

Burgess, J (1984) *Human Factors in Forms Design*, Chicago: Nelson.

Cutts, M and Maher, C (1981) 'Simplifying DHSS letters and forms', *Information Design Journal*, 2, 1, 28–32.

Frohlich, D M (1987) 'On the re-organisation of form-filling behaviour in an electronic medium', *Information Design Journal*, 5, 111–28.

Frohlich, D M and Luff, P (1990) 'Applying the technology of conservation to the technology of conversation', in Luff, P, Gilbert, N and Frohlich, D M (eds) *Computers and Conversation*, London: Academic Press.

Furth, D (1981) 'An investigation of the success of re-designed supplementary benefit documents', *Information Design Journal*, 2, 1, 33–43.

Hartley, J, Davies, I and Burnhill, P (1977) 'Alternatives in the typographic design of questionnaires', *Journal of Occupational Psychology*, *50*, 299–304.

Harvey, L (1987) 'Factors affecting response rates to mailed questionnaires: a comprehensive literature review', *Journal of the Market Research Society*, *29*, 3, 341–53.

James, S, Lewis, A and Allison, F (1987) *The Comprehensibility of Taxation: A study of taxation and communication*, Aldershot: Avebury.

Jansen, J H (1985) 'Effect of questionnaire layout and size and issue involvement on response rates in mail surveys', *Perceptual & Motor Skills*, *61*, 139–42.

Wright, P and Barnard, P (1975) 'Just fill in this form: a review for designers', *Applied Ergonomics*, *6*, 4, 213–26.

Commonly used words and phrases with some alternatives to choose from

The list below is from a shortened version of the thesaurus of abstract and simpler terms presented in *The Good Forms Guide*, published by the British Department of Health and Social Security (1983). It is reproduced with permission of the DHSS and the authors, David Lewis and Jane Castor-Perry. Readers are reminded that the list contains only suggestions and that the alternative terms will not be appropriate in every case.

accede to – agree
accompanying – with
accordingly – so
acquaint – say; tell
acquire – get
adequate – enough
adjustments – changes
advantageous – useful; helpful; better
advise – say; tell
affected – made a difference; changed
aggravated – made worse
alternatives – choices; others
anticipate – expect
apparent – clear; obvious
appropriate – right; proper
approximately – roughly; about

begin – start
on behalf of – for
beneficial – useful; helpful

calculate – work out

in case of – if
cease – finish; stop
commence – begin; start
complete – fill in
component – part
conceal – hide
concerning – about
in connection with – about
consecutive – following on
as a consequence of – because
consider – think
construct – make
consult – talk to; see; moot; ask
convenient – suitable

decrease – make less
defer – put off; delay
delete – cross out
demonstrate – prove; show
denote – show; be
desire – want
diminish – lessen
disclose – tell; show
discontinue – stop; end

dispose – get rid of
distinguish – show; point out
duration – time

economical – cheap
eligible – can get; have the right
    to get
employment – job; work
enable – allow
to enable us – so that we can
enclosed – inside; with
endeavour – try
enquire – ask
ensure – make sure
entitled to x – have the right to
    (get) x
equivalent – equal; the same
erroneous – wrong; false
estimate – work out
exceptionally – only when; in this
    case
excessive – too much
excluding – apart from; not
    including
exclusively – only
expect – think

facilitate – help
feasible – possible
foot of the page – bottom
for the purpose of – to
to forward – to send

generally – usually
on the grounds that – because

henceforth – from now on
hereby – now
herein – here
heretofore – until now
however – but

immediately – now; at once
to implement – to carry out; do
in as much as – because
in case of – if; if there is
in connection with – about; for
in excess of – more than
in lieu of – instead of
in order to – to; so that
in respect of – about

in the course of – while; during
in the event – if
in the neighbourhood – near;
    about
in the near future – soon
incapable – cannot
incapacitated – unable to work
income – money that you have
    coming in
independent – not part of
indication – sign
individual – one; person; you
infirmity – illness
inform – say; tell
initiate – start; begin
inspect – look at; check
irrespective of – whether or not;
    even if
it is felt that – I/we feel/think
it is suggested that – I/we
    suggest

liable to – have to; may have to
locate – find

maintain – keep; look after
maintenance – keep; upkeep;
    looking after; care
mandatory – must
marginal – small
maximum – the most
minimum – the least
miscellaneous – other
modify – change

necessary – must
necessitate – need; require
negligent – not taking enough
    care
nevertheless – but
notify – tell
notwithstanding – even though
numerous – many

obligation – duty
obsolete – out of date
obtain – get
occupation – job; work
occur – happen
option – choice
otherwise – if not

overleaf – on the other side of this page

particulars – details; facts
payable – may/can be paid; can be cashed
pending – until
performed – did
permit – let
come into possession of – get
practically – almost; nearly
prescribed – set; fixed
prior to – before
proceed – go
procure – get
profession – job; work
prolonged – for a long time
promptly – quickly
provided that – if; as long as
purchase – buy

qualifying (period) – the time that matters
quote – say; give

re – about
in receipt of – get; getting
receive – get
reconsider – think again
recoverable – get back; which we can get back
redeemable – can be used; can be cashed
with reference to – about
in regard to – about
regarding – about
regulation – rule
relevant – is important; matters
remedy – cure; answer
remuneration – pay
report – tell
represents – shows; stands for; is
request – ask
require – need
reside – live
residence – where you live; home; house
in respect of – about; for
restriction – limit
resuming – starting again

retain – keep
retention – keeping
return – send (back)
revenue – income; money coming in
revise – alter

select – choose
settlement – payment
signature – sign here
so far as . . . is concerned – about
space is not sufficient – there is not enough room
state – say; tell us; write down
statement – information about; details of
statutory – legal; by law; set down by law
straightaway – now; as soon as it happens; as soon as you can; at once
submit – send
subsequently – later
subsidized – helped
sufficient – enough
supplementary – extra; more

tenant – person who pays rent
terminate – stop; end
therefore – so
to date – so far; up to today
together with – and
transform – change; alter
transmit – send
transpire – happen

ultimately – in the end; at last
unable – cannot
undertake – agree to
utilize – use

verification – proof
vocation – job
voluntary – by choice

whether – if
wholly – all; completely; fully
with a view to – to
with reference to/with regard to – about

11 Text design for the visually impaired

In this chapter I report some of the current research on presenting text for visually impaired readers. I discuss large print, the setting of Braille and how one might improve instructional audiotapes. I also outline some of the advantages and limitations of new technology for presenting text to the visually impaired.

The 1991/92 annual report of the UK Royal National Institute for the Blind (RNIB) claimed that most printed information was inaccessible to people with impaired sight because the print was too small, too faint, or badly designed. It was argued that a great deal could be done to help such people – and countless others who find print difficult – by paying attention to these matters. It was argued this was both easy to do and inexpensive.

In this chapter I shall first present some background information on the size and nature of this problem. I shall then discuss how the ideas that I have put forward in this book can be applied to the presentation of large print, Braille, and audiotape materials. Finally, I will indicate how advances in technology can help and hinder in this regard.

Background

During 1986/87 the RNIB conducted a survey of the needs of blind and partially sighted adults in Britain, and a final report was published in 1991 (Bruce *et al.*, 1991). A similar report on the needs of blind and partially sighted children was published in 1992 (Walker *et al.*, 1992).

The 1991 report indicated that there were approaching one million (960,000) blind and partially sighted adults in Great Britain, many more than those actually registered (239,000). The prevalence rates (for those registered) were as follows:

    3 per 1,000 amongst 16–59-year-olds
   23 per 1,000 amongst 60–74-year-olds
 152 per 1,000 amongst those over 75 years of age.

Thus one person in seven aged 75 or over was blind or partially sighted, and this prevalence rate was almost certainly higher among those over 80 and those over 85.

It is, of course, important to realize that the great majority of these people are partially sighted. The RNIB 1991 report estimated that only

20 per cent of blind people are completely blind (and this number includes people who can perceive light but nothing more). Thus 80 per cent of the blind have varying degrees of visual impairment and, as we shall see below, many can read large print. The main additional sources of information for the visually impaired are:

1. Personal readers (colleagues, friends, family members).
2. Tape recordings.
3. Braille text.
4. New technology.

Similar findings were presented in the 1992 report on blind and partially sighted children. It was estimated that there were at least 100,000 children in Great Britain with significant visual impairments, and possibly as many as 250,000. As many as 80 per cent of the children in the sample were reported to have had their sight problems from birth.

For some children (and adults for that matter) spectacles, contact lenses and other magnifying devices mean that they can in fact read and write using print rather than Braille. In this children's sample:

- over 80 per cent used tape recordings for learning and/or entertainment;
- 40 per cent could read normal size print;
- 63 per cent were using microcomputers in school;
- 36 per cent were using microcomputers at home;
- 90 per cent liked listening to the radio and listening to and watching television.

The RNIB 1991/92 annual report points out that the needs of blind and partially sighted children are complex. More than half of them have additional disabilities, and many such children cannot use Braille or computers because of additional learning or physical difficulties. Although many partially sighted children can read large print, there is only a limited amount of such material available for them. Children who need to use Braille are a small majority, so this means that producing Braille for them is expensive.

Large print

The RNIB considers that 9.5 point type (as used in this book) is too small for many readers, not just the blind and partially sighted. They recommend 12 point type for most documents and 14 point as the minimum type-size for material intended for the blind and partially sighted. (They also recommend sans-serif typefaces for small blocks of instructional text.) Other recommendations are given in Box 11/1.

Box 11/1

Recommendations when designing text for the visually impaired.

- **Contrast**
  There needs to be good contrast between the type and the paper on which it is printed or photocopied. Contrast is affected by paper colour, print colour, type-size and weight.
  Black type on white or yellow paper gives a very good contrast. Pale coloured papers provide better contrast than dark ones. Black, or very dark coloured print can be used if the paper is very pale.
  The print should not run across photographs or illustrations.
- **Type-sizes**
  14 or 16 point is acceptable when printing for the partially sighted (see the text).
- **Type-weights**
  Light type-faces should be avoided, especially in small sizes. Medium and bold type weights are more appropriate in this context.
- **Type-faces**
  Most type-faces in common use are suitable. Bizarre or indistinct type-faces should be avoided. Numbers need to be printed clearly: blind and partially sighted people can easily misread 3, 5, and 8 in some faces, and even 0 and 6.
- **Capital letters**
  Avoid presenting long strings of text in capital letters as they are harder to read than lower case ones.
- **Line-length**
  This, ideally, should be in the range of 50–65 characters. Blind and partially sighted people may prefer shorter lines than this. Avoid hyphenating words at the ends of lines. Do not fit text around illustrations.
- **Spacing**
  Keep to regular word-spacing: do not stretch or condense lines of type, that is, avoid justified type-settings. Allow the line-spacing to be equivalent to the type-size plus the word-spacing. Use a line space between paragraphs, and use space to show the underlying structure of the text. Additional lines or 'rules' may help keep separate unrelated sections. It is worth noting that blind and partially sighted people often need more generous space on forms for hand-written responses as their handwriting tends to be larger than average.
- **Paper**
  Print on glossy paper can be difficult to read. Very thin papers also cause problems because text can show through from the reverse.

Guidelines adapted (and occasionally slightly modified) from RNIB (1993) *See it Right: Clear print guidelines. Fact Sheet 2*, and reproduced with permission of the Public Policy Office, RNIB, 224 Great Portland Street, London W1N 6AA.

It is important to remember, of course, that with large print the width of the text expands, as well as the depth. This may make it difficult to perceive the syntactical groupings of words if the page size (or screen-size) stays the same. Readers may judge here the effects of simple enlargement for themselves, as this section has been printed in 12 on 14 point type.

So, simply enlarging a text may not always be a sensible solution to the problem: one might take the opportunity to reconsider its design. Figure 11/1 shows how the form of a bank statement was altered when it was redesigned to appear in a large print format.

Figure 11/1

How one might re-design a bank statement for visually impaired readers when considering larger print. (Figure reproduced with permission from John Gill.)

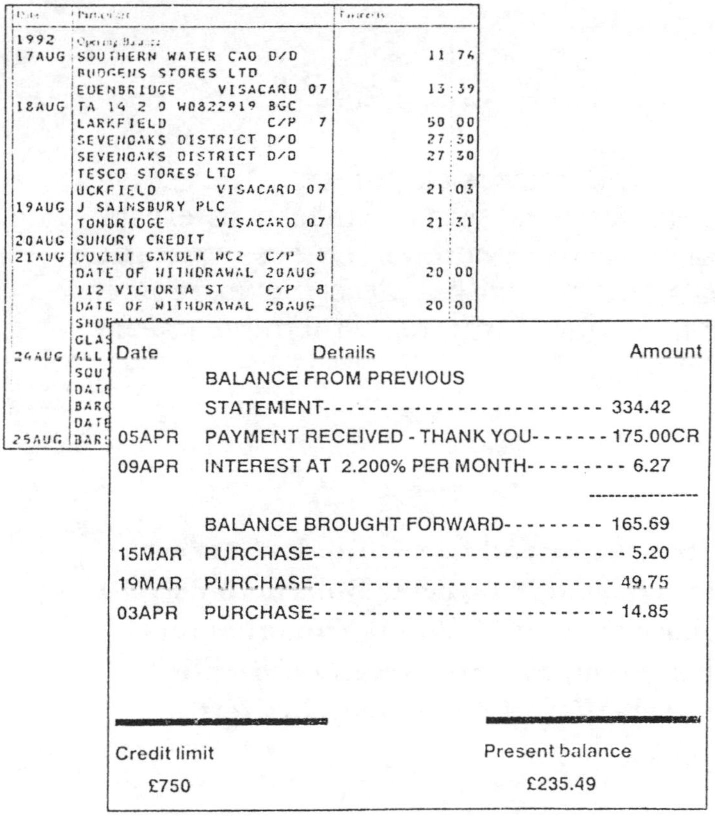

There have been few studies of designing printed texts for the partially sighted, and those that have been carried out have mainly been concerned with the setting of children's reading books rather than with material for adults. Shaw (1969) provides a good review of the earlier literature and reports on a detailed study with adults. Shaw asked her participants to read aloud short passages which varied in type-faces (Gill and Plantin), type-sizes (from 10 point to 24 point), weight (bold and medium) and with various spatial settings (see Figure 11/2).

Figure 11/2

An example of the materials used in Shaw's (1969) experiment. (Figure reproduced with permission from the Library Association.)

Note that the experimental design meant that each participant read only four out of a possible 32 typographic settings.

Bad pairs introduce local babies. Regular villages regard difficult accidents. Your camps pray most affairs. Personal summers feed popular gardens. Average waters love private centres. Sudden gates rule middle

Face:	GILL
Weight:	BOLD
Size:	12 POINT
Spacing:	extra space between letters and words

Old dates advance sick forests. Necessary skies find artificial gifts. Sincere interests show gay roads. National horses write dull leaves. Hungry bridges describe expensive farmers. Reduced minds remember merry

Face:	PLANTIN
Weight:	ROMAN
Size:	14 POINT
Spacing:	extra space between words only

Cheap battles intend fast animals. Scarce presences base fair owners. Both actions seem changed people. Wandering quarters miss fierce connections. Green doors play elder streets. Familiar movements settle

Face:	PLANTIN
Weight:	BOLD
Size:	12 POINT
Spacing:	extra space between lines only

Every advantage lays warm elections. Dear notes aim observed thoughts. Grand visits support various rates. Left journeys read either thing. Managed steel believes sore wives. Fancy productions account delivered

Face:	GILL
Weight:	ROMAN
Size:	14 POINT
Spacing:	"normal"

Table 11/1

The relative legibility of typographic factors in Shaw's (1969) experiment. (Table reproduced from Shaw, 1969, with permission of the Library Association.)

Size*
larger	more legible
smaller	less legible

Weight
bold	more legible
medium	less legible

Face
Gill (sans serif)	more legible
Plantin (serif)	less legible

Spacing
close set	most legible
extra leading	more legible
extra word spacing	less legible
extra letter and word spacing	least legible

Size/Weight
Smaller Bold or Larger Medium	increase
Larger Bold or Smaller Medium	decrease

Face/Weight
Plantin Medium or Gill Bold	increase
Gill Medium or Plantin Bold	decrease

* Readers read two sizes – 12 and 14 point, or 14 and 16 point, or 16 and 18 point, or 18 and 20 point, or 20 and 24 point – according to their reading acuity.

Table 11/1 summarizes the main findings. Shaw reports that an increase in type-size achieved a 16 per cent improvement in reading performance, an increase in weight 9 per cent, and a change from Plantin (a serif face) to Gill Sans (a sans serif face) a 4 per cent improvement. (This type-face change was particularly helpful for readers over 50 years of age.)

These results, of course, must be considered with some caution in view of the fact that:

● the participants read the text out loud;
● they read the materials in experimental conditions;
● the materials were very odd (see Figure 11/2); and
● the data depend on time measures recorded to the nearest tenth of a second by the investigator.

Braille

The Braille system – where each character is conveyed by one of six embossed dots in a 2 × 3 matrix – is well known to many and is illustrated in Figure 11/3. Braille text was originally produced on thick card, but today it is more likely to be produced by a thermoform system with heated paper-thin, plastic sheets. This system also allows one to produce tactile maps and line drawings.

Figure 11/3

A page of Braille text.
(Photo courtesy of
John Coleman.)

It is difficult, of course, for sighted readers to imagine what it would be like to be blind and reading Braille text. One way to do this might be to take a half-way step. Imagine, for instance, reading this chapter by means of a small hole (say 2cm × 1cm) in a large piece of cardboard. The reading of the words would not be substantially different: the problem would lie in finding one's way about and in grasping the underlying structure. The cardboard would effectively prevent one from judging the length of lines and paragraphs and the role of headings and subheadings. It would mask many of the familiar typographic devices that sighted readers take for granted.

Now let us complete the step. Imagine reading this chapter by means of a hole so small that all one can perceive is one or two letters at a time. This might be the equivalent of learning to read Braille text. There is no overall structure, only a linear message to interpret.

To the sighted reader a page of Braille may look like a large and cumbersome equivalent of a piece of conventionally printed text. But this would be naive. Completely blind readers cannot see the top and the bottom of the page simultaneously – they have to work out which is which. They cannot see headings and subheadings at a glance. They cannot see at a glance how many paragraphs there are on the page, and thus how dense the text is. They cannot tell until they start whether the language of the text is going to be easy or difficult. To discover what is there, blind readers must start at the beginning and work through to the end without knowing (for the most part) when the end is coming.

Table 11/2 lists some of the differences between Braille and print and there are several articles available which compare Braille and printed text (see, for example, Poole, undated). Table 11/2 shows that there are many devices for doing things (particularly conveying structure) in print but that Braille may be regarded as impoverished in this respect. What then can be done to reduce this poverty? How can the work I have described in this book help?

Table 11/2

A comparison between printed and Braille text.

	Printed text	Braille text
No. of characters	over 90	maximum 64[1]
No. of typefaces	several	one
No. of different typesizes	several	two
No. of different weights	at least three	one
No. of coloured inks and coloured papers	many combinations	not relevant
Capital letters	yes	no (in UK)
Italic script	yes	no[2]
Underlined script	yes	no[2]
Standard page-sizes	yes, but more of them	yes
Marginal headings	possible	unlikely
Running heads	possible	possible
Paragraphing	indentation line-space	indentation line space three-space paragraphing[3]
Hyphenated words	yes	yes
Justified text	yes	yes
Unjustified text	yes	yes
Position of page numbers	variable	top right
Fixed baseline	variable	usually
Contents pages Indexes References Footnotes	varied formats	standard formats which do not correspond at all closely with print

1. Some characters can have different meanings, dependent on the context.
2. Braille cannot appear in italic or be underlined as such. Normally a sign is given to indicate that the following text is in italic or underlined. If the text is short, then only one sign is given. If the text is long (more than three words) then the sign is doubled, and there is another single sign before the last word.
3. Three-space paragraphing involves leaving three spaces in the line and starting the new paragraph after these (on the same line).

In this book I have focused on how instructional text can be improved by paying attention to the typographic layout, to the wording or language of the text, and to the use of headings, summaries, numbering systems and other such devices (see Chapter 6).

Much of this research would seem applicable to the setting of Braille text. Many Braille texts seem to be devoid of clear spatial cues – perhaps because of the assumption that there is no need to include space because blind people cannot see it – but it would seem to me that the structure of Braille texts could be clarified by the methods discussed in previous chapters. My observations of skilled Braille readers indicate that they can indeed 'look ahead' by quickly scanning (with both forefingers), and that they welcome devices such as headings (Hartley, 1989).

Blind readers require practical information (eg, telling them how long an article is going to be) and contextual information (eg, the use of overview summaries). If headings are numbered and phrased in the form of questions (eg, who, what, when, where, why, how . . .) then blind and visually impaired readers can read with such questions in mind and they will know when they have reached the end of particular sections. Overview summaries and headings enable readers to 'look ahead' more easily, and thus to reduce their memory load whilst reading.

In addition, it might also be profitable to think of how one can convey information differently without the array of typographical devices available in printed text. In Figure 11/4, for instance, I contrast the traditional sequence used in presenting references in a scientific journal with what might be appropriate in a Braille version. In Version A – the traditional setting – the text is continuous and different sections of the references are denoted by different typographic cues. In Braille versions of this material it is conventional to follow this continuous sequence of the printed version. However, in Version B, I have shown how, by re-sequencing the elements and by placing the key elements on different lines, the text is easier to search even though it has no typographic cues. Clearly, making changes such as these may be costly in terms of the additional space required but such changes may be more cost-effective.

At present, of course, we do not know whether re-spacing traditional Braille settings would be of value to blind readers: it may make little difference to those blind from birth. However, it is likely that those who become blind in later life and who wish to learn to read Braille do carry with them a repertoire of expectations about text layout which is currently not realized in Braille.

Version A

Kanski, J. J. and Packard, R. B. S., *Cataract and Lens Implant Surgery,* Churchill Livingstone, 1985, 60pp, £26.00, ISBN 0 443 03205.

Gilbert, P., *Mental Handicap: a practical guide for social workers,* Community Care, 1985, 130pp, pbk £3.95, ISBN 0617 00447 1.

Dechesne, B. H. H., Pons, C. and Schellen, A. M. C. M. (eds.), *Sexuality and Handicap: problems of motor handicapped people,* Woodhead-Faulkner, 1985, 234pp, pbk £19.95, ISBN 0 85941 231 8.

Holloway, C. and Otto, S., *Getting Organised,* Bedford Square Press, 1985, 70pp, pbk £4.95. ISBN 0 7199 1162 1.

Version B

Cataract and Lens Implant Surgery,
    Kanski, J. J. and Packard, R. B. S.
    Churchill Livingstone, 1985,
    60pp, £26.00, ISBN 0 443 03205
Mental Handicap: a practical guide for social workers,
    Gilbert, P.
    Community Care, 1985,
    130pp, pbk £3.95, ISBN 0617 00447 1.
Sexuality and Handicap: problems of motor handicapped people,
    Dechesne, B. H. H., Pons, C. and Schellen,
    A. M. C. M. (eds.),
    Woodhead-Faulkner, 1985,
    234pp, pbk £19.95, ISBN 0 85941 231 8.
Getting Organised,
    Holloway, C. and Otto, S.,
    Bedford Square Press, 1985,
    70pp, pbk £4.95, ISBN 0 7199 1162 1.

Figure 11/4

Version A shows an excerpt from a list of references as typically presented. Version B shows the same text using space rather than typographic cueing to show the structure of the entries in the list. The first entry is now the title, the second one the author(s), the third the place of publication, and the last details of the length, the price and the ISBN number. The argument is that Version B would be more helpful in Braille than Version A.

Instructional audiotapes

It may seem somewhat of a digression to discuss the presentation of instructional audiotapes in this book on printed text but I do this on two grounds:

1. Audiotapes, after all, are usually based upon printed scripts; and
2. Audiotapes are widely used by visually impaired people.

Different sources of audiotapes currently available for visually impaired people are:

1. RNIB's Talking Book Service
2. RNIB's Rapid Reading Service
3. Local talking newspapers
4. Commercial tapes (eg, from banks, airlines, etc.)
5. Locally based 'home-made' tapes.

Talking Books. The RNIB offers a talking books service. The books are recorded professionally in studios (often by well-known speakers), and these can be played back on special recorders supplied by the RNIB. (New machines, to play compact discs, are under consideration.)

Rapid Reading Services. The RNIB has the facility to record books or extracts from them and other materials at very short notice. The readers making the recordings are volunteers, and may not be familiar with the content of the text they are recording.

Local Talking Newspapers. Most cities and many towns have a talking newspaper service. The Talking Newspaper Association of the United Kingdom (TNAUK) is a national, voluntary, non-profit organization which provides audio recordings of over 900 newspapers, journals and magazines.

Commercial Tapes. Many commercial sources provide tapes for the visually impaired. The tapes are professionally produced, feature well-known speakers, and musical support.

Home-made Tapes. These tapes are produced by non-professionals for use in their own contexts. Some, such as those produced by the Open University, are more professional than others, but they may not have professional speakers, or speakers who are familiar with the topics they are reading about.

It may be helpful to think of audiotapes as spoken versions of written scripts. Thus, if the principles of text design advocated in this book are applied to the production of these scripts, this should improve them. To the resulting basic text one can add distinctive audio features, such as different voices for main text and examples, for headings, for questions, or for making asides. One can add music to embellish the text, to introduce and to conclude it. But, as in printed text, it is probably wise not to overdo these variations.

Many instructional audiotapes include tabular and diagrammatic materials, and this presents particular difficulties for both sighted and visually impaired listeners (Hartley, 1991). In recording such materials it is conventional for the speakers to record all the details of the published text, and it is not conventional for them to simplify or re-write the textual materials themselves. Such procedures almost inevitably overload the listeners' memory.

(Few publishers of audiotapes seem to acknowledge how helpful it would be to combine print and audio systems. As we have noted, many visually handicapped people can read large print and many have friends who can help. It would seem sensible, then, to produce packages of text and tape rather than to rely on either system alone.)

There seem to be at least four sources of difficulty in recording instructional audiotapes. Here I shall mention each one in turn, although, of course, they may combine. These are:

1.   Poor quality recording/speaking.
2.   Poor quality original text: badly written text can only confuse listeners.
3.   Poor quality original tabular and illustrative materials: such materials are hard to convey orally. Large tables and complex graphs present particular difficulties.
4.   Poorly prepared speakers: tapes with speakers reading text they do not understand are not helpful.

At present there is a growing interest in the production of instructional audiotapes. A Confederation of Tape Information Services (COTIS) has been formed in the UK, and a number of guidelines have been produced by them. A similar service is provided by the US National Braille Association. There is clearly a need for greater standardization in the conventions to be used in the production of such tapes and for agreement on the fact that the speakers can be free either to add helpful material to aid an author's exposition, or to delete or simplify material that is just too complex to convey on tape.

It would be nice, too, to impart the notion of evaluation into the preparation of audiotapes. Simply trying them out on small groups of appropriate listeners before finalizing them would undoubtedly lead to marked improvements.

Developments in electronic text

There have been several developments in the production of electronic text which have been of interest to people working with the visually impaired and, of course, to the visually impaired themselves. In this section I note some examples, and point to some limitations and advantages.

Steuben and Vockell (1993) point out that one of the most simple developments is, of course, the ability to re-format any text that is entered into a desk-top publishing system. This means that text can be produced in different type-sizes (as appropriate for individuals with different degrees of impairment) and in an unjustified format to ensure equal word spacing. Such an individualized format can be stored as a style sheet or template for a particular person. This means that any text entered into the computer for this person can be almost instantly re-formatted and displayed on screen or on paper in that format.

Hinton (1993) describes recent developments in the field of tactile and audio-tactile diagrams. A current major difficulty with tactile diagrams is that they are often annotated and labelled in Braille and this Braille script takes up considerable space (often more than the diagram). Hinton describes one solution to this difficulty, known as the NOMAD system: here the software is arranged so that audio messages are attached to certain locations on the diagram and they can be vocalized on request.

A major development in text design for the visually impaired lies in this ability to translate text from one medium to another. Some variations on this theme are as follows:

1. Printed text can be inputted into one machine (possibly via optical character recognition technology) to emerge as vibro-tactile Braille at another. The reader keeps his or her finger on the output as it passes by.

2. Printed text can be printed out in a Braille format, and Braille input can be printed out in a paper or screen version.
3. Using word processors with voice output devices allows the text to be heard as it is produced.
4. Voice input devices are beginning to be successfully developed. Here people can speak into a microphone and the sound is translated into words that can be edited, saved and printed out in Braille or traditional text. Voice input devices can also be used instead of a keyboard or mouse input to operate personal computers.

Another area of potential development lies in the advent of compact discs. The amount of text that can be stored on a compact disc is enormous: encyclopaedias, volumes of newspapers, databases of all kinds, etc. Scanning large printed databases is extremely difficult for the partially sighted, but the new technology enables them to do this much more quickly. Any item located can be saved on computer disc and then printed out in print or Braille. Voice synthesizers and software to magnify the text may also be added. (However, the current trend to include more pictorial information on compact discs might cause problems for the visually impaired and users of synthetic speech because, apparently, illustrated compact discs cannot always be used with synthetic speech.)

Finally, we may note here the advent of electronic talking newspapers. Kelway (1993) describes developments in the 'paperless' newspaper provided in the UK – an audio-electronic version of *The Guardian*. An extract from Kelway's description is given in Box 11/2.

These illustrations point to several potential advantages for visually impaired adults and children arising from the development of new technology. The availability of cheap personal computers has been a major step forward in helping visually impaired people to gain access to and to process the same information that is provided to sighted persons.

However, the present-day introduction of graphical user interfaces may well cause problems. Such interfaces require good eyesight to recognize and locate words, boxes, on-screen buttons and icons. Pointing to these images often requires a pointing-based input-device like a mouse. Clearly such graphics-based operating systems pose severe obstacles to visually impaired computer users, and people who find the screens hard to see may be unable to operate the system.

Thus the developments described above require considerable attention to be paid to their design features for presenting information to visually impaired users. Currently the dialogue method of keyboard/mouse and screen dominates the field. But this approach is highly dependent on vision. In the future, however, this approach may be just one possibility among others. Burger and Sperandio (1993) present some interesting discussions of these ideas.

Box 11/2

An extract from Kelway, P (1993) 'The paperless newspaper'. Extract reproduced with permission from the author and *The British Journal of Visual Impairment.*

The flow of information starts at the *Guardian*'s offices where the newspaper text leaves the composing rooms and is prepared for transmission via telephone link to Data Broadcasting International. There the compressed and encrypted data are transferred by land line to the TV companies which then transmit the information in the same way as normal TV programmes. In the subscriber's home, a TV aerial is connected to the computer unit containing the special decoder board and the voice synthesiser, if the latter is required. The computer is left on during the transmission; a time switch can be used to ensure that this causes minimum inconvenience. The transmission takes about twenty minutes. At any time after transmission has been completed, usually at breakfast time, the subscriber can instruct the computer to convert the files received into the form needed for reading. This operation is automatic and takes about five minutes.

The versatility of the system is enormous. Once the transmitted information has been stored on the subscriber's computer, a variety of operations can be carried out. The majority of these can be selected by pressing one of a small number of keys on a control pad. After a particular section of the paper has been chosen, the headlines can be browsed through until an article of interest is reached, simply by pressing the appropriate key. When the article has been selected, pressing another key will make the computer read the first paragraph. Each time the same key is pressed the computer will read the next paragraph until it has finished reading the article. The mode of reading can be changed from paragraph to characters, words, lines, sentences or the entire article.

Summary

1. Many blind and partially sighted children and adults can in fact read large print.
2. Braille text can probably be improved if attention is paid to using space to convey structure, and to using devices such as introductory summaries and numbered headings to help readers keep track of where they are.
3. The scripts for instructional audiotapes can be improved by paying attention to the strategies advocated in this book for improving written communication.
4. The presentation of some materials (such as tables, graphs and illustrations) presents particular difficulties in instructional audiotapes. It would be helpful to combine tapes with written materials to overcome these problems.
5. New technology has the capacity to help greatly visually impaired people in terms of providing instructional materials, but much of this technology is currently vision-orientated.

References

Bruce, I, McKennell, A and Walker, E (1991) *Blind and Partially Sighted Adults in Britain: The RNIB survey Vol. 1*. London: HMSO.

Burger, D and Sperandio, J-C (eds) (1993) *Non-visual Human Computer Interactions: Prospects for the visually handicapped*, Montrouge, France: John Libbey Eurotext.

COTIS (Confederation of Tape Information Services) 79 High Street, Tarporley, Cheshire CW6 OAB.

Hartley, J (1989) 'Text design and the setting of Braille (with a footnote on Moon)', *Information Design Journal*, 5, 3, 183–90.

Hartley, J (1991) 'Presenting visual information orally: some comments on the design of tables, graphs and diagrammatic information and tape-recorded instructional materials for the visually handicapped', *Information Design Journal*, 6, 3, 211–20.

Hinton, R A (1993) 'Tactile and audio tactile images as vehicles for learning', in Burger, D and Sperandio, J-C (eds) *Non-visual Human Computer Interactions: Prospects for the visually handicapped*, Montrouge, France: John Libbey Eurotext.

Kelway, P (1993) 'The paperless newspaper', *The British Journal of Visual Impairment*, 11, 2, 63–4.

National Braille Association (1979) *Tape Recording Manual*, 3rd edn, National Library Services for the Blind and Physically Handicapped, Library of Congress, Washington, DC.

Poole, W (undated) 'Braille as an autonomous script', paper available from the author, BAUK, 97 New Bond Street, London W1.

Shaw, A (1969) *Print for Partial Sight*, London: The Library Association.

Steuben, S and Vockell, E L (1993) 'Reformatting text for learners with disabilities', *Educational Technology*, XXXIII, 6, 46–50.

Talking Newspaper Association of the UK, National Recording Centre, Heathfield, East Sussex TN21 8DB.

Walker, E, Tobin, M and McKennell, A (1992) *Blind and Partially Sighted Children in Britain: The RNIB survey Vol. 2*, London: HMSO.

Suggested further reading

Blenkhorn, P and Calderwood, D (1992) 'Access to personal computers using speech synthesis: a review of the past decade', *New Beacon*, LXXVI, 898, 185–8.

Hartley, J (1988) 'Using principles of text design to improve the effectiveness of audiotapes', *British Journal of Educational Technology*, 19, 1, 4–16.

Hartley, J (1992) 'Communicating diagrams orally', *British Journal of Visual Impairment*, 10, 1, 37–8.

Hartley, J (ed.) (1992) *Technology & Writing: Readings in the psychology of written communication*, London: Jessica Kingsley.

Marsland, D (1992) *Read All About It: Newspapers for blind people*, Centre for Evaluation Research, Lancaster House, Borough Road, Isleworth TW7 5DU.

Petrie, H L and Gill, J G (1993) 'Current research on access to graphical user interfaces for visually disabled computer users', *European Journal of Special Needs Education*, 8, 2, 153–7.

Shaw, A (1968) 'Print for poor-vision readers', *The Penrose Annual*, 61, 92–101.

Ungar, S, Blades, M and Spencer, C (1993) 'The role of tactile maps in mobility training', *British Journal of Visual Impairment*, 11, 2, 59–61.

Vanderleiden, G C (1991) 'Graphic user interfaces: a tough problem with a net gain for users who are blind', *Technology & Disability*, 1, 1, 93–9.

12 Instructional text and older readers

This chapter discusses some of the difficulties facing older readers of instructional text. I first outline research with older readers and relatively simple text settings, and I then describe research with more complex materials. Finally, I consider new technological developments in this context.

The proportion of older people in society has gradually been increasing throughout the twentieth century. Life expectancy at birth in the UK has increased by 50 per cent in this century and 4 in every 10 British adults are now over 50. In the United States currently 12 per cent of the population is 65 years of age or older and the number of Americans over the age of 65 years is expected to double to 65 million by the year 2030.

Thus people are living longer and the number of elderly people in the community is getting larger. Consequently there are more older people reading traditional texts, and more texts being produced especially for them.

The research on the effects of ageing can be described in terms of three overlapping areas: physiological, cognitive and social. Physiological research looks at the biology of ageing and its physiological correlates. Most people, for example, experience a sharp decline in eyesight and the effects of this are amplified in Table 12/1. Cognitive research on ageing focuses on changes in memory, learning and judgement. Such effects have implications for work on text design. Social research on ageing examines how societies expect their older members to function. Studies of 'ageism', for example, focus on how commonly held attitudes and

Table 12/1

The relationship between age and problems with eyesight (Office of Population Censuses & Surveys, 1982).

	Age 65–69 %	Age 70–74 %	Age 75–79 %	Age 80–84 %	Age 85+ %
People who do not wear glasses	4	3	3	4	4
People who wear glasses, but have no difficulty seeing	78	77	68	65	51
People who wear glasses, but still have difficulty seeing	18	20	30	32	45

beliefs about what old people should and should not do determine to a considerable extent what, in fact, they do do.

It is difficult to summarize in a few lines the main findings of studies of ageing and their implications for text design. Nonetheless, for the sake of argument, I would like to suggest two main points which I think it is helpful to bear in mind when thinking about these issues. It is generally accepted that:

- working memory capacity (ie, information held and used in ongoing tasks) declines as people get older, and
- the more difficult the task and the older the person, the more disproportionately difficult the task becomes.

Studies of memory for text suggest that a number of possibilities can occur. Evidence has been provided in different studies indicating that:

- older people sometimes remember the main ideas but forget the details;
- older people sometimes remember the details but forget the main ideas; and
- older people sometimes forget both the main ideas and the details.

These different outcomes may result from different investigators focusing on different issues in their studies. The findings suggest that older people may not have much difficulty reading or working with text that is relatively simple (in terms of its typography) or familiar to them. However, text which is typographically complex and which deals with unfamiliar material (like how to operate a video recorder) may cause middle-aged and older people considerable problems.

Thus one might not expect differences between older and younger readers when the verbal ability of the readers is high, when they have good prior knowledge, and when the texts are well presented. Differences, however, might well be expected to emerge with less-able readers, less familiar materials and poorly designed text.

Improving typographically simple layouts

Generally speaking, the literature reviewed above suggests that text will be easier for older people to use if their perceptual and memory processing loads are reduced. I would want to argue that this can be achieved by, for example:

- using larger type-sizes;
- using more readable text;
- using clearer layouts; and
- clarifying the structure of the text by, for example, using summaries, headings and 'signals'.

In this first section of this chapter I shall outline the results from a review of some of the studies specifically carried out with older users in these respects. These studies have mainly used what I call typographically simple text – that is, continuous expository prose. I shall discuss studies with typographically complex text in the next section.

When preparing to write this chapter I reviewed some 18 studies which had examined various aspects of text design with older users. Unfortunately, as shown in Table 12/2, there was an insufficient number of studies in each category for me to be able to make any clear generalizations from their conclusions. Table 12/2 shows the number of studies found for each aspect of text design:

Table 12/2

Number of studies	Text design feature
5	Type-size
4	Unjustified text
2	Underlining
2	Improving readability
2	Advanced organizers
1	Questions in text
1	Signals
1	Text structure and organization

However, all five studies on type-size did suggest that larger type-sizes were more suitable for older readers, and 12 or 14 point type seems reasonable, in line with the RNIB's recommendations mentioned in the previous chapter.

The four studies with unjustified text suggested that there were advantages for unjustified text with *less-able* older readers when the line lengths were short (seven to eight words).

The two studies on underlining and the two on advanced organizers had mixed results – one positive and one neutral in each case. The two studies on improving readability showed that this had no effect with age. However, there were age effects for the studies with questions, signals and variations in text structure: older readers did less well than younger ones, but both groups were helped by the textual variable being considered.

My review highlighted three issues in this research:

1. There were ability effects rather than age effects in about half of these studies. Here more-able participants did better than less-able ones, irrespective of age.
2. Less than half of the 18 studies used a control group of younger participants: most were done with a single group of older persons. So it was not possible to see if the variable in question was additionally helpful (or not) for older readers.
3. Only one of the investigators reported working with text that was appropriately designed for visually impaired older readers (although one or two others did check that their participants could

read the texts). Thus, one might argue, many of the older readers in these studies were probably working under an additional handicap.

Typographically complex texts and the older reader

So far I have discussed research with texts which have had a relatively simple typographic structure. I now turn to studies of older people using more complex materials. Such materials include, for example, bus and train schedules, labels on medicine bottles, food packaging, and government forms. In this section of this chapter three examples are presented. The findings suggest not only the difficulties for older people, but also some solutions.

Income tax forms

In the UK, unlike most other countries, tax is deducted at source from earnings throughout the tax year. It is expected that the right amount will be deducted at the right time and that this will continue throughout the tax year. Thus, at the end of the tax year, it is assumed that the correct amount of tax has been deducted and that there is no need for any further action. Accordingly, most people do not complete annual tax returns. Checks are, however, made, typically on a three-yearly basis, with a very complex form. This system is different from that of many other countries including, for example, the USA, where most people assess their own income tax liability and file a return by a particular date every year.

Senior citizens have particular difficulties with such forms and so do people who help them to complete them. One person writes thus:

> My recollection of trying to sort out my mother's tax returns, which I did every few years, was that her problem was that (a) she couldn't find any of the relevant papers from her bank etc., (b) she couldn't remember anything; and (c) she kept on putting off writing business letters for a few months more in the hope that she would die before they really insisted on an answer. I was reduced to writing accompanying letters to the Revenue telling them that while she had signed the form they could not assume she understood anything on it.

James *et al.* (1987) provide a comprehensive report on the difficulties of both ordinary and senior citizens in completing such forms, and they present data from several comparison studies. Here I shall restrict my account to one or two of their findings from their work with senior citizens. In one such study one particular form for such people was redesigned: the introductory notes were made clearer (see Figures 12/1a and 12/1b). Questions on the form were asked in a more consistent manner and the text layout was revised.

Figure 12/1a

A section from the original income tax form studied by James *et al.* (1987)

About this notice of coding
This notice cancels any previous notice of coding for the above year.

As your pension is being increased from 22 November 1982 the allocation of allowances has been changed as shown overleaf. As your net allowances are less than your National Insurance pension, an ordinary code will not deduct sufficient tax so I am giving you a special code. After 22 November 1982 your employer or paying officer will use this code to deduct tax from your pay or pension from a previous employment. The effect of the new code is that you will pay more tax. In general the extra tax on the pension increase will be 30%. If your pay or occupational pension is increased the code will also collect the tax on that increase.

Figure 12/1b

A revised version of the above. (Reproduced with permission from James *et al.*, 1987.)

About this Coding Notice
From 22 November the National Insurance pension is being increased. Since this pension is taxable, your code number has been changed so that the right amount of tax is deducted from your other pension or pay.

This means that the deductions on your other pension or pay include the tax payable on your National Insurance pension. If this were not done, you would have to pay the tax on your National Insurance pension separately.

In another study with another form the authors assessed the effectiveness of the changes made with (i) studies of individuals and (ii) a postal survey. In the study with individuals, 71 per cent of the respondents reported that they would have difficulty completing the original form, but this figure was reduced to 53 per cent for the revised one.

The kinds of difficulties these respondents commented on were as follows:

	Original form (N=88)	*Revised form (N=56)*
Reading	27%	23%
Writing	25%	36%
Understanding	28%	21%

James *et al.* also revised the introductory notes to accompany this new form: 81 per cent of the respondents found the revised notes helpful, compared with 64 per cent for the original notes.

The results from the postal survey showed little difference between the complaints and difficulties of respondents who completed this particular form annually. However, the results indicated that the revised version of the form was superior for people who did not complete tax forms every year, for women respondents, for single taxpayers and for members of 'low income households'.

James *et al.* report in much more detail on the problems of tax forms generally, and specifically those for senior citizens. They make numerous suggestions about how such forms could be improved, and about how one might study the effectiveness of changing their design. They also discuss the implications of such changes for such a large organization as the UK Inland Revenue which, they report, handled 8,163 different forms in the tax year 1980–81, and printed 11,000,000 copies of one of the particular forms studied by James *et al.*

Procedural instructions

Morrell and Park (1993) surveyed the literature on the effectiveness of procedural instructions for assembly tasks. In this survey they noted that, although the findings suggested that realistic, text-relevant illustrations did help people to carry out such tasks, none of the studies involved had included older participants. The authors anticipated that elderly respondents would find such procedural tasks difficult to do because of their reliance on working memory.

In their study, Morrell and Park asked a group of young adults (aged 18 to 30 years) and a group of older adults (aged 60 to 75 years) to take part. They were each provided with an instruction booklet for building two practice figures and nine experimental figures out of Lego blocks and pieces of foamboard. These figures varied in complexity. There were three different instructional booklets: text only, pictures only, and both text and pictures. The written instructions were printed in 18 point on 24 point bold.

The results indicated that performance was affected by age, instructional format, and level of complexity. The younger adults consistently out-performed the older ones with each of the three instructional formats. The text and pictures together format reduced the error rate for both of the age groups compared to the other formats. The difficulty of the task had a greater effect on the elderly than it did on the young adults.

These findings suggest that the design of this kind of instructional material is not simple: readers, tasks and formats all need to be considered. However, the findings do suggest that older adults can do such tasks, even if not quite as well as young ones and that instructions can be written to help them. Morrell and Park suggest that additional subsets of instructions need to be prepared for the more complex tasks which might be tackled by older persons.

Flow charts

A number of researchers have concluded that continuous text is probably not the best vehicle for expressing complex inter-related rules, and they have turned to alternative modes of expression, particular the algorithm or flow-chart. An algorithm may be defined as an exact prescription or recipe leading to a specific outcome.

Although algorithms can often be easier to understand than their conventional prose counterparts, it seems that many adults, especially older ones, might be confused by their unconventional appearance. Indeed, this appears to have been one of the findings in a study reported by Michael (1988).

This study looked at the performance of secondary school children (aged 11–12 and 14–15 years) and senior citizens (average age 71 years) solving problems with either the flow chart or the set of contingency statements shown in Figure 12/2 to help them.

Figure 12/2

Top. The flow chart used in the experiment.
Bottom. The contingency statements used in the experiment.

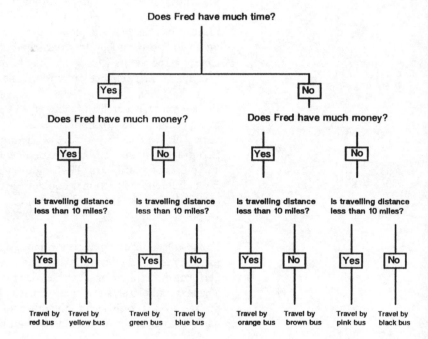

If Fred only has much time (and not much money)
    travel by **green bus** if travelling distance is less than 10 miles;
    travel by **blue bus** if travelling distance is more than 10 miles.

If Fred only has much money (and not much time)
    travel by **orange bus** if travelling distance is less than 10 miles;
    travel by **brown bus** if travelling distance is more than 10 miles.

If Fred has much time and much money
    travel by **red bus** if travelling distance is less than 10 miles;
    travel by **yellow bus** if travelling distance is more than 10 miles.

If Fred has neither much time nor much money
    travel by **pink bus** if travelling distance is less than 10 miles;
    travel by **black bus** if travelling distance is more than 10 miles.

Thus, for example, a typical problem might read:

> Fred is going to the bank. It will soon be time for the bank to close. Fred is carrying a big bag of ten pound notes. He has to travel by bus because he can't drive a car. The bus journey is 18 miles long. *What colour bus does Fred catch?*

After a practice session the participants had to use either the flow chart or the contingency statements to solve eight such problems, and their speed of responding and error rates were recorded over a series of trials.

The results indicated that the school children solved the problems more quickly with the flow charts than with the contingency statements, and that there were clear practice effects. The participants got faster as the trials progressed. However, there were no significant differences in error rates. Here the flow chart and the contingency statements were equally effective.

The picture for the senior citizens was rather different. This time there were no significant differences in speed of responding with the two formats, or in the error rates. However, the speed of responding was much slower for the older participants (double that of the younger ones on the first trial) and the error rates were much higher. The initial error rate for the senior citizens was 75 per cent on the first trial and 58 per cent on the second one (compared with 39 per cent and 29 per cent for the 14–15-year-old school children).

In the discussion of the results of this experiment Michael noted that:

1. Several elderly people did not realise that the flow chart should be read selectively from top-to-bottom, and not from left to right as in conventional text. This caused difficulties for a large number of the older participants, but it was almost unknown amongst the schoolchildren.
2. The elderly participants who could use the flow chart often seemed so pleased that they had got from the top of the chart to the 'decision box' at the bottom that they paid little attention to which channel they took through the flow chart and its relation to the task in hand. They were then confused about how they were supposed to answer the question.
3. There was a worrying possibility that design features of the experiment may have caused extra difficulties. Sometimes the elderly participants chose a bus-colour as directed in the instructions but then justified their choice in ways which indicated that they were not making it in the light of the information provided in the experiment. So, for instance, one participant chose 'green' and justified her choice by saying '. . . if he's got a long way to travel he'll need a Crossville bus' (thus making a reference to one of the local bus companies).

Thus these results suggest that it would be wiser to give older respondents more practice with such materials and perhaps to use more realistic situations.

Conclusions

The three examples provided above give some support to the point made earlier. As the text settings get more complex, then the older and particularly the less-able the reader, the greater the difficulties. The ways of improving complex text settings described above do help both older and younger readers, but perhaps the effect is likely to be more marked with the younger ones. Special additional provision may be needed to help the older ones. In only one of the three studies cited, however, did the investigators take into account the likely visual impairment of their older readers.

Technology and the older reader

There are many additional ways of presenting information apart from text. Audiotapes, video cassettes, compact discs, electronic databases and voice-input devices all provide ways of presenting information which may obviate the need to read. Czaja *et al.* (1993) review the evidence that shows that new technology can be used to facilitate learning, support memory, organize data, and generally improve the quality of life for older people.

None the less, the implication from the research reviewed in this chapter is that more could be done to facilitate this process if what is already known about the effects of ageing were to be incorporated into the design of these materials.

Most studies that involve teaching people to use word-processing packages indicate that it takes longer to teach older learners. As Charness and Bosman (1990) put it, 'computers stress the perceptual, cognitive and motor capabilities of their users'. Elderly people with visual handicaps might find the process more difficult than the younger visually impaired children described in the previous chapter. They could perhaps be helped with larger screens, with more variable print sizes, with the use of black on white lettering on monochrome displays, the elimination of difficult colour discriminations (eg, blue on green, and between colours of the same hue) and the use of simpler keyboards and operating systems.

Indeed, when developing instructional text, one simple rule of thumb might be to ensure that older people are included in tests of initial versions of the text. Designing for the older person may not confuse the young: designing for the younger one may confuse the old.

Summary

1. Research has indicated that older people have difficulties with expository prose and instructional text. Reader variables (such as age and ability), text variables (such as readability and structure) and task variables (what to do with the text) are all important considerations.
2. Research with simple text settings is too diffuse to suggest that those factors which help young readers to process text offer *additional* advantages to the elderly. Curiously enough, few of the relevant studies actually compare the performance of older and younger readers, and none have used texts specifically designed to help the older reader.
3. In studies with more complex text settings (income tax forms, procedural instructions and flow charts) young readers consistently out-perform old ones. Here the elderly may need additional support. In the few studies reported with complex text settings, it is more likely that young will be compared with old, and that age will be taken into account in designing the materials.
4. New technology can facilitate the text processing of the young and the old, but more needs to be done to take into account the ageing process in designing and evaluating these materials.

References

Charness, N and Bosman, EA (1990) 'Human factors and design for older adults', in Birren, J E and Schaie, K W (eds) *Handbook of the Psychology of Aging*, San Diego: Academic Press.

Czaja, S, Guerrier, J H, Nair, S N and Landauer, T K (1993) 'Computer communication as an aid to independence for older adults', *Behaviour and Information Technology*, 12, 4, 197–207.

James, S, Lewis, A and Allison, F (1987) *The Comprehensibility of Taxation: A study of taxation and communication*, Aldershot: Avebury.

Michael, D (1988) 'User differences and graphic design: some studies with flow charts', unpublished PhD thesis, University of Keele.

Morrell, R W and Park, D C (1992) 'The effects of age, illustrations and task variables on the performance of procedural assembly tasks', *Psychology and Aging*, 8, 3, 389–99.

Suggested further reading

Czaja, S (1988) 'Microcomputers and the elderly', in Helander, M (ed.) *Handbook of Human-Computer Interaction*, Amsterdam: Elsevier.

Epstein, J (1981) 'Informing the elderly', *Information Design Journal*, 2, 215–35.

Hartley, J (1994) 'Text design and the older reader: a literature review', paper available from the author, Department of Psychology, Keele University, Staffordshire ST5 5BG.

Kemper, S and Rash S J (1992) 'Speech and writing across the life-span', in Gruneberg, M M, Morris, P E and Sykes, R N (eds) *Practical Aspects of Memory, Vol. 2*, Chichester: Wiley.

Light, L L (1991) 'Memory and aging: four hypotheses in search of data', *Annual Review of Psychology*, 42, 333–76.

Meyer, B J F, Young, C J and Bartlett, B J (1989) *Memory Improved: Reading and memory enhancement across the life-span through strategic text structures*, Hillsdale, NJ: Erlbaum.

Meyer, B J F, Marsiske, M and Willis, S (1992) 'Text processing variables predict the readability of everyday documents read by older adults', paper available from the authors, Department of Psychology, Pennsylvania State University, PA 16802.

Rybash, J M, Hoyer, W J and Roodin, P A (1986) *Adult Cognition and Aging*, New York: Pergamon.

Stordant, M and VandenBos, G R (eds) (1989) *The Adult Years: Continuity & change*, Washington: American Psychological Association.

13 Designing electronic text

▼

This chapter considers how far the findings of research with printed text can be used in the design of electronic text. Electronic text has certain limitations and certain advantages. Here I suggest that electronic text will be easier to use when more attention is paid to the design features discussed in this book.

▲

In this chapter the term 'electronic text' is used to cover text on visual display units (VDUs), cathode ray tubes or television screens (CRTs), and also the printouts of displays from such screens. The aims of this chapter are to consider:

1. How far the contents discussed in the earlier chapters (particularly those concerning the legibility, layout and language of prose) are relevant to electronic text;
2. How conventionally printed and electronic text differ; and,
3. How these differences can cause problems in using electronic text.

The legibility of text on VDUs and CRTs is a function of several additional factors to those we have considered so far with respect to printed text. These factors can be divided into two kinds: traditional and modern. Traditional factors include parameters such as luminance, contrast, character height, character width, spacing between the characters and so on. Modern factors include such things as flicker, glare, refresh rate, drift and resolution, as well as parameters related to CRT size and to stroke and dot-matrix technology. Most of these modern factors are not the main concern of this particular text, but some references to studies of their effects are provided below.

When considering the legibility of text on VDUs and CRTs it is often assumed that all that we know about the design of printed text can be applied straightforwardly to the design of electronic text. In some respects this is the case. Much of what I have discussed in earlier chapters – stressing the need for spatial consistency in layout and the importance of simple language – is directly applicable to electronic text. For example, in my view, it would seem wise to opt for unjustified left-ranging text, to avoid word-breaks, and to use consistent horizontal and vertical spacing to separate and group related parts in the text. Tullis (1988), in an important review of issues related to screen design, states that

> The main point to remember about the placement and sequence of elements on the screen is that the user should be able to develop very clear expectations about what information will fall where.

Tullis makes several useful suggestions about how to determine standard layouts which will help the readers to achieve this.

Limitations of screen-based electronic text

However, screen-based electronic text differs from printed text in many ways. So, in many instances, the assumption that what is true of print is also true of electronic text is (unfortunately) wishful thinking.

Currently, the most important difference between the printed page and the electronic screen lies in the amount of text one can accommodate comfortably on one page or 'screenful'. Generally speaking (although there are exceptions), the amount of text that one can display per screen is much smaller than one can display per page. If, for example, you were reading this on a typical screen that displayed 20 lines of text, each containing 80 characters, then by now you would already be on your fourth 'screenful'.

Not only is the screen grid constricting in terms of space, but also it is differently arranged from that of a typical book page. For example, the usual configuration of the screen is 'landscape' (ie, wider than it is tall) rather than 'portrait' (ie, taller than it is wide). Further complications arise when one starts to use 'windows' in this electronic text: sometimes text is written around windows, sometimes it is covered by them.

Developments in screen design might well remove some of these difficulties. Larger (A4) screen sizes are already available and, indeed, there are even larger split-screen displays with the facilities for inserting footnotes or extra details in space set aside for 'windows' as appropriate.

In this chapter I shall first consider three kinds of problem presented by today's small screen configuration. They are:

1. Problems of legibility: screen-based text is not always easy to read.
2. Problems of search and retrieval: more attention has to be paid to helping readers to know both where they are and how to find their way to and fro in the text.
3. Problems of writing text to match this particular medium: authors have to try to write screen-sized chunks of text, and they face great difficulties incorporating tabular and graphic materials.

I shall then continue to discuss some of the advantages of electronic text.

Reading electronic text

Studies which have compared how well children and adults read electronic text compared with 'hard copy' (printed text) have suggested that people read electronic text more slowly than text presented in the conventional way. However, screen size, the number of characters per line, whether the image is positive (dark characters on a light background) or negative (light characters on a dark background), and screen resolution are important issues here.

Dillon (1992) reviews the evidence which commonly suggests that in comparing reading from screen with reading from text, screen reading is slower, less accurate and more tiring. Dillon concludes that although there is some evidence in support of these allegations, this evidence is equivocal. Often the tasks used (e.g. proofreading) reflect only a limited subset of what can be called reading, and the quality of the screen presentations leaves much to be desired. Indeed, a series of studies by John Gould has shown that the better the image quality the more reading from a screen resembles reading from paper, and that the performance differences described above disappear (see, for example, Gould *et al.*, 1987). None the less, even with excellent image quality, problems do arise – as in printed text. As noted above, these focus on how best to display the text in the limited space available, and how to aid search and retrieval.

Grabinger (1993) has conducted a series of studies in which students have been asked to judge what he terms the 'studyability' of screens taken from computer-based instructional presentations. The participants were asked to compare systematically pairs of 20 screen presentations, to rate them, and to express a preference for one of them in terms of their perceived utility for study. Next they indicated, by marking on a scale, how much more 'studyable' their preferred screen was to the other one. Grabinger's aim was to identify constructs that could guide the design of computer screens used to display information in computer-assisted instruction, hypertext (see below) or on-line help applications.

Grabinger found that three main dimensions affected the results. Dimension 1 was named *interestingness*: the participants liked screens that were attractive, readable, studiable, interesting, inviting and dynamic. Dimension 2 was named *organization*: the participants preferred screens that were neat, clear and organized. Dimension 3 was named *structure*: the participants liked screens that were planned, structured, and controlled. Figure 13/1 shows the most and the least preferred screen in this investigation.

Grabinger's study examined user preferences for different screen designs. The next step is to compare the actual effectiveness of different screen designs. Duin's (1988) study is of interest in this respect. Duin used guidelines from research on document and instructional design to create what she called a 'well-designed' and a 'poorly designed' computer-assisted instructional program for students on a writing course. Figure 13/2 lists a selection of the guidelines she used.

The results of this study showed that students using the 'well-designed' program outperformed students using the 'poorly designed' one, they were more flexible in using it, and they were more involved in and excited about their work.

Figure 13/1

The least and the most preferred screen in Grabinger's experiment. (Figure reproduced courtesy of Scott Grabinger.)

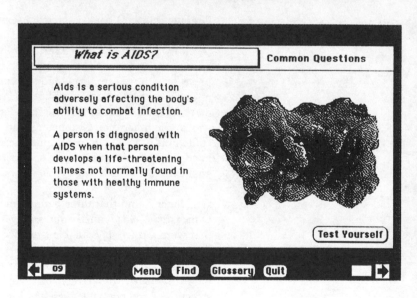

MULTIDIMENSIONAL SCALING (or MDS) is a set of mathematical techniques that enable a researcher to uncover the "hidden structure" of data bases, as illustrated below. The authors, who are among the pioneers in developing and using these techniques, deal very concretely with the problems really faced in using them, and present varied applications.

An example illustrating an interesting MULTIDIMENSIONAL SCALING application in political science involves data from a 1968 election study conducted by the Survey Research Center of the University of Michigan. Each respondent in a national sample evaluated 12 actual or possible candidates for President of the United States. How similarly did the public view the candidates? What identifiable features can we discern in the varying evaluations of the candidates that can help us understand what led individual citizens to their decisions? MULTIDIMENSIONAL SCALING can help answer these questions by locating the political candidates in a spatial configuration or "map." Once we have located the candidates or points in (multidimensional) space, we seek to determine the hidden structure, or theoretical meaning of this spatial reprresntation of candidates.

Applying MULTIDIMENSIONAL SCALING to these data provides a way of reducing the data about 12 candidates to two dimensions representing the

15

What is AIDS?   **Common Questions**

Aids is a serious condition adversely affecting the body's ability to combat infection.

A person is diagnosed with AIDS when that person develops a life-threatening illness not normally found in those with healthy immune systems.

Test Yourself

09   **Menu** **Find** **Glossary** **Quit**

Problems of search and retrieval

Compared with printed text it is difficult, if not impossible, to flip through, or skim an electronic text and to make side-by-side comparisons of different pages. You cannot put your finger in an electronic text to keep your place while you check back on an earlier point. One might imagine, as noted in the previous chapters, that problems such as these will be even greater for older and/or visually handicapped readers.

There are, however, some developments in this respect. In one electronic journal it is possible to keep and compare the top few lines of various pages, and facilities for making notes are being explored. However, the problem becomes acute when the electronic database is large.

Figure 13/2

A selection from the guidelines used by Ann Duin to produce a well-designed computer-assisted instructional writing program.

Conceptual Guidelines

- Determine the goals and objectives of the exercise
- Identify who the student-users will be (their knowledge, attitudes and needs)
- Identify educational strategies (individual and collaborative work, process work, open-ended questions, and appropriate examples)
- Develop two levels of questions – questions to stimulate critical thinking and questions to aid the students in phrasing actual components of documents.

Linguistic Guidelines

- Use simple language except when describing specific concepts
- Avoid acronyms, abbreviations, jargon and sexist examples
- Keep the overall tone informal.

Visual Guidelines

- Keep text densities below 50% of characters available on the screen
- Keep the bottom left area of the screen free as a cueing area
- Keep line lengths to 60 characters or less
- Place text in single-column format
- Keep the right margins unjustified for the most part
- Break lines at ends of words rather than hyphenating
- Place blank lines around blocks of text
- Place blank lines between paragraphs if text is not already broken up.

Movement Guidelines

- Keep the number of commands needed to move through the exercise at a minimum
- Place cues in consistent areas
- Use simple and consistent graphics to cue students to the beginning of sections
- Highlight major sections at each stage of the project
- Indicate the amount of time it will take students to complete a section.

A common discussion point in conferences on hypertext/hypermedia (see below) is how to prevent users from being 'lost in hyperspace'.

Many researchers suggest the use of running headings (as in books) to indicate where one is and numbered paragraphs to aid search and retrieval. Running headings, of course, occupy space – space which is at a premium in electronic text. The use of such headings may mean that only about three-quarters of the screen (or less) remains for the information itself.

Attention also has to be paid to the design of indexes and contents pages to help the users find their way about the text. Such pages list topics and sub-topics and readers have to select appropriately from them. It is conventional to structure such 'menus' in a hierarchical or 'tree-like' manner with the basic or primary choices first, and the lower-level, more detailed choices later, but a simpler way might be to list all the entries alphabetically.

The difficulty with the former arrangement is that choices deemed appropriate by the author may not match what the reader has in mind, making search difficult. Furthermore, the author has to choose between providing a few detailed (and crowded) menus, or a larger number of less detailed (but spacious) ones that will take the reader time to work through. It may well be that once readers are familiar with the system they will prefer a few detailed menus to lots of simple ones.

A new consideration in this area arises from developments in hypertext (see below). Readers can progress (or diverge) by using selectable buttons (which are hidden from view). By selecting a particular key word, for example, readers are taken directly to linked nodes of information. This ability to 'point and go' has distinct advantages over paging, or specifying 'go-to' jumps on a menu.

In comparison studies of search tasks using printed and electronic text, the results have not been very clear. It appears, for example, that people search electronic text more slowly but more carefully than they do printed text, and certainly large differences have been reported between search strategies of experts and novices.

It would seem worthwhile, therefore, to pursue the idea that people might process electronic text differently from printed text. If there are differences, then we can consider changing the design of the presentation either to accommodate or to enhance them. One of the virtues of electronic text compared with print is that we can manipulate more easily what we want different readers to do by making such texts much more interactive.

Problems of writing for electronic text

One way of resolving some of the difficulties presented by small screen configurations is to write text in smaller sections, to characterize such sections by headings, to number the headings and the paragraphs in each subsection, and to allow readers to pick and choose the sequences in which they will read the text by using a menu of section headings. In writing for electronic journals I have noted how I have been forced to number paragraphs and to use headings much more frequently so that readers can have this opportunity.

This procedure works reasonably well if the headings match readers' expectations or accepted practice. Scientific articles, for example, are (normally) clearly structured. There is usually an abstract, introduction, method, results, discussion, conclusion and reference section – in that order. An electronic text presentation of such an article allows readers to select which parts they wish to read in whatever order they choose. However, it is more difficult to organize text which is less coherent.

Tabular and graphic materials pose additional problems for electronic text. The nature of the system being used often means that graphics appear crude and amateurish, although some systems are better than others. None the less, even technically superior systems can have deficient graphics. Sometimes there are too many lines per graph, and three-dimensional presentations are often used instead of simple two-dimensional bar charts. Regular readers of financial information will know that comparisons between items (eg, currencies) that have gone up or down relative to one another are difficult to grasp if they are presented in graphs that ascend and descend from a zero baseline.

Small screen configurations make it difficult to present complex tabular and graphic materials, especially if one wants to add captions and/or explanatory text. However, colour and animation are important considerations here and these will be discussed further below.

The structure of tables in electronic text has to be as simple as possible and related to the way in which the tables are to be used. Because of the limits in space it is tempting to use abbreviations for row and column headings, but undoubtedly such procedures cause difficulties for readers. Once, when I was preparing an article for publication in an electronic journal, I decided that I had three options for dealing with a complex table. I could (a) divide it up into three separate tables, (b) simplify it by excluding lots of detail, or (c) simplify it and let the reader know that more details were available in a series of tables in a later appendix. I chose option (b). The point I am making here is that much material may have to be excluded from electronic text if small screens persist. Indeed, many of the illustrations used in this book could not appear today on the majority of screens if they were to be presented in electronic form.

Compensating features

Storage capacity

So far the discussion has proceeded as though electronic text has few redeeming features compared with print on paper. It is worth pointing out, therefore, that the main virtues of electronic text are (i) that it does not use paper storage facilities, and that vast amounts of information can be stored in computer databases at (relatively) little cost, and (ii) that such text need not be read in the order in which the author presents it.

With conventional text the paperwork can simply become too cumbersome. One study of a technical manual found that, in order to diagnose and repair one aircraft radar malfunction, a technician had to refer to 165 pages in eight documents and to look at 41 different places in these documents! One of the main benefits of electronic text is that it can accelerate access to such information. Systems can be devised which help the users to look for and to sift the information that they require. What is important about these systems is that what the readers see is much less than what they do not see.

Such systems are commonly used in so-called 'hypertexts'. Jonassen (1989) defines hypertexts as 'collections of text fragments' rather than continuous prose. He explains,

> These text fragments are tied together by links. Hypertext is not meant, like most texts, to be read from beginning to end. It would be possible I suppose to read a small hypertext in that way, but by and large readers make continual choices about where they will go and what they will read next.

Figure 13/3 shows the contents page from the print version of Jonassen's book *Hypertext/Hypermedia*. If you turn to, say, page 5 to study the characteristics of hypertext you will find another circular 'hypermap'. Now you can choose to read any one of 14 text fragments in any order you decide. And, when reading these fragments, you can cross-refer to other 'pages'. The main topics, if you like, are nodes (or points of departure for several different issues) and each node and issue has connecting links across the text. This kind of text is different from the familiar branching texts of programmed learning: there you had to read in a particular sequence, even if you occasionally branched to and fro along the way.

Figure 13/3

The contents page for Jonassen's *Hypertext/ Hypermedia*. (Figure reproduced courtesy of Educational Technology Publications.)

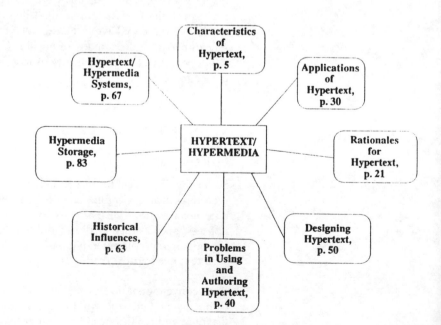

Hypertext/Hypermedia contains about 90 A4-size pages of text fragments. Its purpose is to explain and demonstrate the notion of hypertext using printed text as its medium. However, most current exemplars of hypertext are computer-based and information is presented on an electronic screen. This gives them immediate advantages and disadvantages over Jonassen's printed format. The advantages are that one can store many more text fragments in a far less bulky fashion and that one can make connections and links almost instantaneously. The disadvantages are that, as noted above, reading text on screen is not the easiest of procedures and that it is difficult to keep one's place.

So, like Jonassen's paper hypertext, computer-based hypertexts contain textual information which is stored in nodes connected by links, but they do so on a grander scale. Computer-based hypermedia can contain textual, graphic, and audiovisual data stored on video and compact discs.

Dynamic presentations

Hypertexts can have additional advantages. Mitre's *Guide to the Literature on Human Computer Interaction* (Fox, 1989) takes the voluminous set of guidelines on this topic published by Smith and Mosier (1986) and presents them in a computer-based hypertext. As noted above, this reduces the bulkiness of the text and allows for easy cross-referencing. But this hypertext does more than this. On one left-hand page of the *printed* text version, for example, there is an illustration of a poorly designed table, and an improved version of the same table is presented on the facing right-hand page (rather like my examples in Chapter 7).

The printed text explains the procedures followed to improve the table (such as re-sequencing the elements to meet the user's needs, re-spacing the columns to clarify the contents, and the introduction of line-spacing at appropriate intervals to aid searching along the rows). In the *hypertext* version, however, the screen presents the original table, and the reader is invited to see how the table will change when any one of these procedures is applied. The readers are thus able to see before their very eyes how the clarity of a table can be enhanced by the application of a specific guideline or a combination of them. In other words, whereas most printed texts can only show 'before' and 'after' examples, the hypertext adds to the printed text by illustrating dynamically what happens when you apply particular guidelines for improving text, both separately and in combination. This enhances understanding.

Levels of text

Another feature of the new systems worth pointing out here is the ability to 'hide' text below invisible 'buttons' that can be activated by (say) a mouse pointer. This makes it possible to create texts with different amounts of content or detail. In writing this book, for instance, I debated with myself whether or not to provide detailed references to the research literature which would support or offer different viewpoints on what I was writing about at the time. The scholar in me wanted to document every point: the writer in me said the resulting product would be difficult to read! But I could achieve both aims if I were writing an electronic text: I could, for instance, place a button behind every researcher's name, or any sentence that starts, 'the research shows ...'. Interested readers could then click on to these parts of the text to reveal the supporting references, or even a more detailed discussion.

The use of colour

One of the most important features of electronic text is the availability of multi-coloured formats. In some systems many colours are used, but in the British information systems *Ceefax*, *Oracle* and *Prestel*, which parallel the North American *Telidon* or *NAPLPS* systems, only seven colours are used (although each can form the background for the others). These colours are green, red, blue, magenta, cyan (pale blue), yellow and white. The research suggests that green, white, yellow and cyan are the most useful colours to use for text on a dark background.

In the same way that italic or bold print might be used in conventional text, colour cueing can be used to emphasize particular words or phrases (eg, red for DO NOT ...). Colour can be used to indicate categories of importance, as in the News on *Ceefax*, where the main paragraphs appear in white and subparagraphs in blue. Colour can be used in place of space to convey organization and structure. Thus rows or columns in tables (or groups of them) may be presented in alternating colours to aid retrieval. Studies show, however, that the resulting 'striped' effect can cause great difficulties if readers are expected to read both down and across the tables.

One particular problem with using colour cueing to convey text structure is that (unlike spatial cueing) there does not appear to be an intuitive range of colours that would suggest a hierarchy of importance. In addition, if colours are to be used in a meaningful way then the users must be able to distinguish between the functions of different colours and thus colour coding must not be excessive.

It cannot be emphasized too strongly that the use of colour facilities must be restrained in eletronic text. Questions should always be asked concerning the functional and educational purpose of any additional colour.

The research suggests that the number of colours used on any one graph or chart should be kept to a minimum, that they should be used consistently, and that they should be clearly differentiated from other colours used in the wording of items on the screen. Further technical problems arise from the fact that warm colours (red and yellow) usually appear larger than cooler (green and blue) and that, for example, a bar presented in one colour in a bar chart may seem larger or smaller depending upon the background colour on which it is presented.

Sound and graphics

Noisy animated graphics are compulsive features of video games and no doubt such features can be used to advantage in electronic text, particularly with handicapped users. Sound can be added to vision to provide reinforcement for success in instructional programmes, for example. Such graphics are now becoming common in training packages.

A number of writers have pointed to the value of animation for showing cyclical changes, such as the operation of the internal combustion engine. Graphics can be used like film to show sequential processes and to build up understanding step-by-step.

As noted above, at present graphics in electronic text often appear crude and amateurish because of the nature of the system being used. However, developments with high-resolution screens can be expected to reduce this problem. Studies of the effectiveness of animated graphics in electronic text have largely, but not always, testified to their value (see, for example, Alesandrini, 1987). A study by Reed (1986) suggested how different strategies in producing graphics can have different effects. Graphics that were successful in Reed's experiments –

- replaced rather than supplemented verbal components;
- drew the readers' attention to salient features of the topic under discussion; and
- required the user to interact with the material.

Inter-relating text and graphics

It is quite common, in both printed and electronic text, to find text 'wrapped around' a graphic. I know of no research on this particular matter, but my experience would suggest that such a presentation might be confusing (especially if the graphic is an animated one in an electronic text).

In Chapters 8 and 9, when discussing printed text, I suggested that graphic and illustrative materials should be positioned near to their textual reference. As noted then, this recommendation is difficult to follow when there are large graphics, or a series of graphics with very little text between them. However, the aim is to reduce the need to look ahead, or back, in order to follow the text that is being read.
This problem can be minimized in printed text by a careful use of the double-page spread. In electronic text, of course, it may be accentuated by the reduced dimensions of the screen 'page'. Just where to position text and illustrative materials that won't fit on the same screen is a considerable problem. Two solutions (which do not appear to be used as much as they could) are to supply printed workbooks with illustrative materials to accompany electronic text, and, conversely, to supply electronic graphics to accompany printed text.

Alesandrini (1987) pays particular attention to interactive animated graphics and graphics application software. With these tools, learners can create their own computer graphics using input devices such as a mouse or joystick:

> Images can be enlarged, flipped, rotated, animated, duplicated, colored, sized up or down, moved around the screen, deleted, and more – all without the learner having to program the system.

Alesandrini reports that this flexibility is especially evident in the creation of colour graphics. Learners can try out varieties of different colours simply by pressing different function keys. So, just as word-processing has changed the nature of writing and editing text, graphics application software is revolutionizing the process of preparing artwork.

Working with VDUs

At present there have been few studies which have examined the effects of doing lengthy instructional tasks on a VDU and compared them with other methods (such as textbooks). There is some evidence that suggests that working uninterrupted for long periods of time with VDUs is likely to produce complaints of eyestrain, headaches and tiredness, particularly if the image quality is poor. It is, of course, difficult to know whether these complaints arise from working with VDUs, or from the fact that any job which requires individuals to remain in the same position, to focus on a fixed plane, and to concentrate for a long time without rest is likely to cause feelings of strain and tiredness. It is likely, however, that VDUs with poor image quality do contribute to these strains. No doubt many of the symptoms can be accounted for by inappropriate ergonomic factors, such as screen glare caused by too high a lighting level, inappropriate seating and working positions, as well as by ocular defects. None the less, research does suggest that inappropriate interline spacing may well lead to headaches (Wilkins, 1991). It would be agreeable to think that the strain of using VDUs could be reduced by using better designed instructional text.

Summary

1. The legibility of electronic text is a function of many interacting variables in addition to those of printed text.
2. The research on printed text suggests that the legibility of electronic text will be enhanced if the text is set unjustified and presented with consistent horizontal and vertical spacing to group and separate the relevant parts.
3. However, the presentation of electronic text is constrained at present by small grid configurations and limited graphics resolution. These produce problems both for readers and designers. Readers find it difficult to skim and find their way about such text. Designers find it difficult to present tabular and graphic materials. Such features can restrict the advantages of hypertext.
4. The use of colour is an additional feature but a number of considerations have to be borne in mind if colour is to be used effectively.
5. The difficulties that readers experience when using VDUs for extended periods of time might be reduced by the use of better designed textual displays.

References

Alesandrini, K I (1987) 'Computer graphics in learning and instruction', in Houghton, H A and Willows, D M (eds) *The Psychology of Illustration, Vol 2: Instructional issues*, New York: Springer-Verlag.

Dillon, A (1992) 'Reading from paper versus screens: A critical review of the empirical literature', *Ergonomics*, 35, 10, 1271–95.

Duin, A H (1988) 'Computer assisted instructional displays: Effects on students' computing behaviors, prewriting and attitudes', *Journal of Computer-Based Instruction*, 15, 2, 48–56.

Fox, J (1989) 'Dynamic rules for interface design', paper available from the author, The Mitre Corporation, Bedford, MA 01730, USA.

Gould, J D, Alfaro, L, Finn, R, Grischkowsky, N and Minuto, A (1987) 'Reading from CRT displays can be as fast as reading from paper', *Human Factors*, 29, 5, 497–517.

Grabinger, R S (1994) 'Model vs real screen perceptions: newer judgements', *Educational Technology, Research and Development* (in press).

Jonassen, D H (1989) *Hypertext/Hypermedia*, Englewood Cliffs, NJ: Educational Technology Publications.

Reed, S K (1986) 'Effect of computer graphics on improving estimates to algebra word problems', *Journal of Educational Psychology*, 77, 3, 285–98.

Smith, S L and Mosier, J N (1986) *Guidelines for the Design of Interface Software*, Technical Report ESD-TR-86-278, Bedford MA 01730: The Mitre Corporation.

Tullis, T S (1988) 'Screen design', in Helander, M (ed.) *Handbook of Human-Computer Interaction*, Amsterdam: Elsevier.

Wilkins, A (1991) 'Visual discomfort and reading', in Stein, J F (ed.) *Vision and Visual Dyslexia*, Basingstoke: Macmillan.

Suggested further reading

Barker, P G (1993) *Exploring Hypermedia*, London: Kogan Page.

Barker, P G (ed.) (1991) 'Electronic books', special issue of *Educational Training & Technology International*, 28, 4, 269–368.

Billingsley, P A (1988) 'Taking panes: Issues in the design of window systems', in Helander, M (ed.) *Handbook of Human-Computer Interaction*, Amsterdam: Elsevier.

Clarke, A (1992) *Principles of Screen Design for Computer-Based Learning Materials* (2nd edn), Moorfoot, Sheffield: Employment Department.

Galitz, W O (1993) *User-Interface Screen Design*, Wellesley, MA: QED Publishers Group.

Helander, M (ed.) (1988) *Handbook of Human-Computer Interaction*, Amsterdam: Elsevier.

Milheim, W D (1993) 'How to use animation in computer-assisted learning', *British Journal of Educational Technology*, 24, 3, 171–78.

Norrish, P (1984) 'Moving tables from paper to screen', *Visible Language*, XVIII, 2, 154–70.

Paap, K R and Roske-Hofstrand, R J (1988) 'Design of menus', in Helander, M (ed.) *Handbook of Human-Computer Interaction*, Amsterdam: Elsevier.

Palmiter, S, Elkerton, J and Baggett, P (1991) 'Animated demonstrations versus written instructions for learning procedural tasks: a preliminary investigation', *International Journal of Man-Machine Studies*, 34, 687–701.

Rubin, M M (1985) 'Spatial context as an aid to page layout: A system for planning and sketching', *Visible Language*, XIX, 2, 243–50.

Spenkelink, G P J, Besuijen, K and Brok, J (1993) 'An instrument for the measurement of the visual quality of displays', *Behaviour and Information Technology*, 12, 4, 249–60.

14 Evaluating instructional text

▼

Instructional text can be evaluated in a number of different ways. In this chapter I discuss evaluation in terms of content, presentation and teaching effectiveness. Case-histories are provided to indicate the value of the approaches to design advocated in this book.

▲

How can we evaluate instructional text? What questions must we ask and how can we answer them? The literature in this area reveals a concern with at least three main – but related – areas of enquiry. We can ask questions about a text's content, about the way it is presented (in terms of its typography and layout), and about its teaching effectiveness. Within each of these areas we can ask further questions about the methods available to help us make decisions about the value of a particular piece of instructional text.

How can we evaluate content?

We can approach the task of evaluating the content of written materials from different points of view. If we are assessing for our own needs a book such as this one then our main concerns will be with our likely use of it. As potential readers we will be concerned with whether or not the content is sufficiently relevant for our purposes and sufficiently interesting for us to read it in detail. We will also want to consider whether or not we should *buy* the book. However, if we are choosing a textbook for our students we will be concerned with whether or not the content will meet our teaching objectives. We will also want to see if there are outdated materials and important omissions or biases of any kind – academic, national, racial and sexual. In addition, we will also be concerned with the depth and breadth of the book and how much we may need to supplement it with other materials.

This much seems obvious, but it is not obvious how to be sure that the content meets such qualifications. Not only are the above descriptions hard to specify but also, at times, they may be misleading. Users of technical documents sometimes complain, for instance, that such documents contain *too much* information; that is, there is more than is needed for a task to be done. The same kind of problem can arise with textbooks. How much background information, of interest historically but now admittedly out of date, should go into, say, a science textbook? And how can one be assured that bias is not present, except through rather subjective attempts to interpret today's shifting nationalistic, racial and sexual standards?

Evaluating content is at best a difficult activity, and always a subjective one. However, one way to increase objectivity is to increase the number of judges and to provide some sort of checklist to ensure that all the judges evaluate the same concerns. Figure 14/1 provides an example of part of one such checklist.

Figure 14/1

A checklist for assessing textbooks. (In the original version each item is followed by a five-point rating scale, from very good to very bad.)

A. Format of book

1. General appearance
2. Practicality of size and colour for classroom use
3. Readability of type
4. Durability and flexibility of binding
5. Appeal of page layouts
6. Appropriateness of the illustrations
7. Usefulness of chapter headings
8. Usability of index
9. Quality of the paper

B. Organization and content

10. Consistency of the organization and emphases with the teaching and learning standards of the school
11. Consistency of the point of view of the book with the basic principles of the subject area for which the book is being considered
12. Usefulness in stimulating critical thinking
13. Aid in stimulating students in forming their own goals and towards self-evaluation
14. Usefulness in providing situations for problem solving
15. Usefulness in furthering the systematic and sequential programme of the course of study
16. Clarity and succinctness of the explanations
17. Interest appeal
18. Provision for measuring student achievement
19. Adequacy of the chapter organization
20. Adaptability of content to classroom situations and to varying abilities of individual students
21. Degree of challenge for the reasonably well-prepared students
22. Usefulness for the more able students
23. Usefulness for the slow learners
24. Adequacy of the quality and quantity of skills assignments
25. Provision for review and maintenance of skills previously taught

This kind of approach is commonly used for evaluating school textbooks in countries with state-controlled school systems.
Although such checklists are useful in making the judges' ratings more systematic and consistent, there appear to be no *standard* tools that have been widely adopted: different evaluators tend to make up their own questionnaires. Farr and Tulley (1985), for instance, reported that the average number of items on the checklists that they studied was 73: the longest had 180 items and the shortest 42.

Such checklists are usually completed *before* recommending a particular textbook for use, but there is, of course, no reason why such information could not be collected *after* the texts have been used by readers and by teachers. Information gained in this way would be useful in deciding whether or not to use the book again, and it would be helpful to authors who are planning subsequent editions. Such feedback sheets can occasionally be found in scholastic textbooks and academic journals.

Furthermore, there is no reason why such checklists cannot be completed *during* the production of a text. Chapters can be tried out in draft form before publication, and readers can complete feedback forms on chapters as they read them. The information gained can be provided to authors, who can use it when they are finalizing their chapters.

How can we evaluate the typography and layout of the text?

As shown in Figure 14/1, checklists used for evaluating school textbooks often contain items that require judges to rate the technical quality of the texts as well as their content. Generally speaking it is difficult, without expert knowledge, to evaluate some of the precise details of layout and typographic practice. None the less, it is possible to look out for some more obvious problems. Questions might be asked, for instance, concerning the density of the type (are the lines too close?) and the excessive use of typographical cues such as bold and italic, and typefaces of different sizes (does it look too messy?). When considering the density of the type it is appropriate to bear in mind that readers like text to be spaced out and organized so that they can perceive its underlying structure at a glance.

I have tried in this text to indicate how my approach to the design and layout of instructional materials might help instructional effectiveness. Figure 14/2 provides a summary checklist of the sorts of things (in terms of typographic decisions) that I would look for when evaluating a text typographically. I have framed each question so that an answer 'yes' indicates a positive response.

How can we evaluate teaching effectiveness?

Perhaps the most common question asked about a piece of text is how suitable or appropriate it is for its intended readers. Sometimes, when the target audience is known well, arriving at the answer is a relatively easy task. However, if the text is to be used by multiple users for a variety of different purposes, then the task becomes more difficult.

Several methods can be used to evaluate the suitability of a text for its intended audience. Most measures can be used by *authors* when they are producing their own text (to ensure that it is effective) and by *judges* when they are assessing the suitability of published text for others. Let us consider some of them in turn.

Figure 14/2

A checklist for the evaluation of typographic decision making in instructional materials.

Organization of content

☐ Are the chapter divisions sufficiently clear?
☐ Are there summaries of the chapter content?
☐ Are the heading levels coded clearly and consistently?
☐ Are the subsections within the chapters differentiated clearly and consistently by the spatial organization of the text?
☐ Are there running heads at the top of each page?
☐ Is there an author and subject index?

Page detailing

☐ Is the contents page clearly organized?
☐ Are the page numbers provided on the contents page easy to locate?
☐ Are the margins sufficient for binding, filing, etc.?
☐ If there are multiple tables, graphs, pictures, etc. in the text, is a single-column format used?
☐ Is the text set unjustified?
☐ Is hyphenation avoided at the ends of lines?
☐ Does the interrelationship between type-size, line-length, and interline space seem appropriate for the reader?
☐ Is the vertical spacing consistent?
☐ Is the stopping point at the bottom of a page determined by the content?
☐ Are footnotes avoided?
☐ Will the type-faces used withstand repeated copying?
☐ Is typographic cueing used sparingly?
☐ Is the use of colour appropriate and consistent throughout the text?

The role of examples and illustrative material

☐ Does the illustrative material add to the text's instructional effectiveness?
☐ Is the illustrative material placed appropriately in the text, and in sequence within it?
☐ Does the illustrative material have clear instructional captions?
☐ Are the captions positioned consistently throughout the text?
☐ If examples are provided in the text are these clearly recognizable as examples?
☐ If tables, graphs, diagrams and examples are presented in the text, are they clearly drawn so that it is easy to grasp their essential message?
☐ If the text is mathematical are particular problems (eg, equations) presented in a standard way throughout the text?

Readability formulas

As we saw in Chapter 6, readability formulas can be applied to text in order to predict the age at which children, on average, will have the necessary reading skills and abilities to understand it. Most readability formulas in fact are not as accurate at predicting this age as one might wish, but the figures that they provide do give a rough guide. Furthermore, if one uses the same formula to compare two different texts, or to compare an original with a revised version, then one does get an idea of relative difficulty.

There have been several attempts to see whether or not teachers can match the difficulty of a text to a pupil's age or ability without using a readability formula. Klare (1976) showed that the ability to make such judgements varied widely between individuals. However, a group measure (ie, the average of the judgements of a set of teachers) seemed to agree quite well with the measures derived from a single readability formula. It might be wiser, therefore, to use an appropriate readability formula than to rely on individual judgement to assess the difficulty level of various texts.

One particular point to note here is that textbook vocabulary which is considered normal for pupils in the USA or the UK is likely to be more difficult for pupils in developing countries. Indeed, there may be even greater variability in the reading abilities of such pupils. Grade and age levels as determined by current American readability formulas may therefore overestimate the suitability of texts in these situations.

A readability formula provides a *rough* guide to text difficulty. If the score goes off the scale (as is often the case with government documents) then it is clear that the text is too difficult for most readers. But we have to question whether simplicity is all that is required. We may agree that the *Sun* (with its predicated reading age of 12 years) is easier to read than *The Times* (with its predicated reading age of 18 years) but surely we do not agree that the two papers are equal in quality? The results of readability formulas thus have to be weighed against other criteria, perhaps relating to the value and sophistication of what is being communicated.

Furthermore, in order to select a useful text one needs to know not only about the readers' reading skills, but also about their background knowledge, and possibly their motivation. The more learners know about a topic, the more readable a text will be on that topic, and the easier they will find it. And, the more motivated learners are, the more they will persist. None the less, as we noted above, the relative style difficulty of two texts with the same content area can be meaningfully compared with a readability formula, and several studies have shown advantages for more readable texts, particularly with less-able readers (see, for example, Britton *et al.*, 1993).

The cloze procedure

Another method for judging text difficulty that is similar in a way to using a readability formula is the *cloze procedure* (Taylor, 1953). There is one major difference, however, in that in order to use the cloze procedure you have to test the text out with appropriate readers (whereas readability formulas can be applied directly to the text). With the cloze procedure, samples of a passage are presented with, say, every sixth word missing, and the readers are required to fill in the missing words.

Technically speaking, if every sixth word is deleted, then six versions should be prepared with the gaps each starting from a different point. However, it is more common . . . . prepare one version, and perhaps . . . . to focus the gaps on . . . . words. Whatever the procedure, the . . . . are scored either (a) by . . . . accepting as correct those responses . . . . directly match what the original . . . . actually said, or (b) by . . . . these, together with acceptable synonyms. Since the two scoring methods (a) and (b) correlate highly, it is more objective to use the tougher measure of matching exact words. (In the case above these are: 'to', 'even', 'important', 'passages', 'only', 'which', 'author' and 'accepting'.)

Scores can be improved slightly by varying the length of the dotted lines to match the lengths of the missing words, by providing dashes to match the number of letters missing in each word, or by providing the first of the missing letters. These minor variations, however, do not affect the main purpose of this measure, which is to assess the reader's comprehension of the text and, by inference, its difficulty. The cloze procedure has a strong advantage over readability formulas in that it can be used to assess the effects of the presence of other features, such as illustrations or underlining, on the comprehension of text (see, for example, Reid *et al.*, 1983).

Readers' judgements

A rather different but useful measure of text difficulty is to ask readers to judge difficulty for themselves. One simple procedure is to ask potential readers to circle on the text those areas, sentences or words that they think readers *less able or less knowledgeable than themselves* will find difficult. In my experience if you ask readers to point out difficulties for *others* then they are much more forthcoming than if you ask them to point out their own difficulties.

An elaboration of this technique is to use a form of what is called *protocol analysis* (Bainbridge, 1990). Here readers are asked to verbalize out loud what they are thinking about as they are reading or using text, and the recorded output is subsequently analysed. This technique has proved extremely useful in evaluating complex text such as that provided by computer manuals. Some critics of this approach suggest that talking about a task while trying to do it can cause difficulties, and this does seem to be a reasonable objection.

However, such problems can be partly overcome by getting readers to work in pairs to discuss together problems they are facing or by videotaping people using texts and then asking them to talk through the resulting tapes – which can be stopped at any point to allow the readers to make an extended commentary.

In this section of this chapter we may also consider *reader preferences*. In the first edition of this book I dismissed such preferences because I considered them to be 'untutored' judgements. At that time it seemed to me that readers' preferences might be based on inappropriate considerations: for example, a person might prefer a text on the basis of the quality of the paper rather than the content. Today, however, I am not so dismissive of preference measures and, indeed, my own studies of them have shown that they are sensitive to differences between novices and experts. Furthermore, people have clear views about what they like in texts, and how they expect texts to perform. So, first impressions might colour attitudes to texts. A text which looks dull, dense and turgid is not going to encourage one to read it, no matter how important the content. Thus I now use preference judgements as one of the battery of measures in my toolkit. Preference measures can tell you whether one text is preferred to another, whether people see no difference, or whether people prefer one text even though (in your eyes) it is not as effective as the other. This kind of information needs to be considered, together with data provided by other measures.

One useful procedure to use if you wish to compare preferences for a number of designs which vary in different ways is the method of *paired comparisons*. Suppose, for example, you had 15 designs. Using this method you ask a participant to compare design 1 with 2 and record the preference. The participant then compares design 1 with 3, 1 with 4, 1 with 5 and so on, until 1 with 15 is reached and each preference is recorded. Then the participant starts again, this time comparing design 2 with 3, 2 with 4, 2 with 5 and so on until 2 with 15. This procedure is repeated in terms of design 3 with 4, 5, 6 etc., 4 with 5, 6, 7 etc., until all the designs have been systematically compared. Finally, this procedure is repeated with several participants, and then the number of recorded preferences for each design is totalled to see which one has been preferred most often.

Experimental comparisons

All of the measures described above can be used relatively informally: some researchers, however, may wish to carry out more formal experimental comparisons, and to use more precise measuring instruments. Some people, for instance, might be interested in measuring reading speed, or the ease with which people can find information, or the readers' degree of understanding and recall, or their ability to follow the text and to carry out instructions effectively. Some tools might be quite precise – for example, eye-movement recording devices – and some methods might require finely-tuned statistical procedures to tease out significant differences.

Over the last 20 years or so my colleagues and I have used a variety of methods (and combinations of them) to evaluate instructional text experimentally. Some of these methods have proved more appropriate than others in different circumstances. Thus oral reading measures (where the reader reads out loud) can give detailed information about specific parts of the text which create difficulties; search tasks can evaluate the layout of highly structured text (such as bibliographies and telephone directories); comprehension measures can evaluate the effectiveness of continuous prose; and readability and preference measures can provide additional sources of information.

Experimental evaluations of text require one to start off with a specific question, to prepare a variety of text solutions to illustrate it, to select the ones that seem most plausible and practical, and then to evaluate their success by using appropriate measures. Such evaluations are limited because:

1. It is not possible to evaluate and compare every possible solution to a problem;
2. The methods that we have at our disposal for evaluation in this area tend to be somewhat limited;
3. Readers who know that they are taking part in an experiment may behave differently from normal; and,
4. Different measures have their own in-built assumptions.
    (For example, many measures seem to assume that the readers always start at the beginning of a text and read through it steadily to the end.)

None the less, experimental comparisons can provide evidence which is of value in evaluating texts. As a rule of thumb, psychologists believe that experimentally-obtained data are more valuable than are subjective opinions. And this is especially the case when the experimenter (i) uses several measures in combination rather than relying on one alone, and (ii) has replicated the studies.

Improving texts

Sometimes we may not be so interested in making *comparisons* between texts as we are in using the measures discussed above to help us to *improve* them. One of the most useful approaches here involves a process of reiteration. This requires us first to test the text with appropriate readers, and then to revise it on the basis of the results obtained. We then test it again with another set of readers, and then revise it again and so on, until the text achieves its objectives. This iterative approach, which is described in the last of the following case histories, was used extensively in a study reported by Waller (1984).

Costs of production

Finally, attention should be drawn to a rather different kind of measure, not discussed much in this text. This is the *costs* of production. In my experiments I have sometimes shown reductions in the cost of production without any loss in comprehension, and sometimes great improvements in comprehension for a slight increase in cost. These latter results point to the hidden costs of badly designed materials and to the fact that cost effectiveness is an important consideration. And we always need to consider the hidden costs for the users as well as those for the producers of badly designed texts. These issues will be discussed further in the context of the last case history to be presented below.

Case-histories

To complete this chapter I now present four case-histories of evaluation studies. Taken together, these studies indicate the value of following the guidelines presented in this textbook.

Case-history 1. Readability
Consider the following passage:

> The rapidly growing wealth of Britain during the reign of the first four Georges not only brought increased comfort; it also helped to inspire a great achievement in the arts. Later, under Queen Victoria, wealth became widely spread among people who had no family background of culture and little artistic taste, and were therefore liable either to ignore art altogether or to spend money on buildings and pictures of little merit. In the eighteenth century, wealth was still piling up in the hands of the landed aristocracy, who with their great houses and their 'Grand Tours' abroad had by now a traditional interest in art. These noblemen established admirable standards of taste in painting and architecture which others were generally content to follow. And in literature, where authors came to depend as the century progressed not on patronage of an individual nobleman but on the favour of a small cultured upper and upper-middle class, the achievement was no less brilliant.

This passage was found in an old history textbook that was still available for 12- to 13-year-old children to read in Staffordshire schools. The passage has a Flesch reading grade level of 14.5 which suggests that it is more suitable for 19-year-olds than it is for the 12- to 13-year-olds who were supposed to be reading it!

To revise this passage one of my undergraduate students, Christine Williams, carried out the following procedures:

1. She shortened the sentences: for example, long complex sentences were turned into two simpler ones.
2. She replaced unusual words by more common ones: for example 'established' became 'set up'.
3. She replaced metaphorical phrases by literal ones: for example 'under Queen Victoria' became 'in Queen Victoria's reign'.
4. She added phrases which made the digression in time clearer to the reader.

This led to the following passage:

> The wealth of Britain grew quickly in the eighteenth century, during the reigns of the first four King Georges. This caused better living conditions for people in Britain. It also helped to bring about some fine achievements in designing buildings, in paintings and in other arts. Later, in Queen Victoria's reign, wealth became more widespread among ordinary people, who did not come from families which had been interested in the arts for many years. These people were likely either to ignore the arts or to spend money on buildings and paintings of low standard. In the previous eighteenth century it was those born in the already rich land-owning families who had become wealthier. These noblemen, with their grand houses and tours abroad, had a traditional family interest in the arts. They set up high standards of taste in painting and building design which other people followed. As time went by in the eighteenth century the writers of books and poetry also achieved high standards. The reasons for this were not only that the noblemen were interested in their work but also that men from the upper and middle classes took an interest.

This version has a Flesch reading grade level of 11 which suggests that it is now suitable for 16-year-olds.

To assess the effectiveness of this version, children in two classes of 12- to 13-year-olds (one of high and one of middle ability) were given one or other of the two versions of the passage. They were asked first to read their passage for a period of ten minutes and then to write down, as if for an absent friend, the main points of the passage. Independent judges scored these recalls. Making the passage more readable did not have any effect with the able children (Class 1) but it significantly helped the less-able ones (Class 2).

Subsequent studies, using cloze procedures, have also demonstrated that the revised passage is much easier to comprehend than the original. The findings in this case-history are typical of several studies of this kind. It seems as though large differences in Flesch scores are needed for the effects to show themselves, and that more readable text is likely to be more helpful for less-able readers.

It should be noted that some researchers recommend that readability formulas should *not* be used to evaluate or develop texts, the main objection being that it is unwise to use a formula for rewriting text. The argument, which has some force, is that if one just simplifies text by splitting sentences, removing connectives, and simplifying multi-syllabic words, then the resulting text is likely to be stilted, lacking in clear organization and, in fact, harder to read.

Case-history 2. Search tasks
In Chapter 7, Figures 7/5a and 7/5b show part of the original and part of a redesigned version of a leaflet distributed by the British Psychological Society. To test the efficiency of the redesign, both versions were typed

on A4 paper, and then reduced to A5 (thus simulating printed text). The original document covered four A5 pages, and the revised version five A5 pages.

Groups of undergraduate students were asked to carry out a number of search tasks using the two documents. The results were quite conclusive. With the original layout only six out of 23 students (26 per cent) were able to find all the items of business to be discussed at the meeting: with the revised version 18 out of 21 (86 per cent) found them. With the original layout only 12 out of 23 students (48 per cent) were able to find the four special resolutions which were to be discussed, whereas with the revised version 20 out of 21 (95 per cent) found them. The times taken to retrieve these items were significantly faster for students using the revised version.

In this example then, in terms of paper costs, the revised edition of the pamphlet was more expensive. In terms of cost-effectiveness, however, the revised edition was clearly superior.

Case-history 3. *Using multiple measures*

Figures 7/6a and 7/6b in Chapter 7 illustrate an original and a revised version of a page from a technical document. To compare the effectiveness of these revisions to the total document, which was three pages long, five different measures were used. The purpose of this case-history is to show not only how different measures might produce different results, but also how a combination of measures leads to a broader overall picture. The results were as follows:

- In terms of *readability* the first 100 words of the original document (excluding headings) had a reading age level of 19.5 years, whereas the first 100 words of the revised version had a reading age level of 15 years (Gunning FOG index).
- In terms of *reading speed* there were no significant differences between the average times taken by two groups of ten university students to read the three pages set in either version.
- In terms of *factual recall*, however, these same groups of students recalled an average of 5.4 out of 10 for the original and 7.9 out of 10 for the revised version. (This difference is statistically significant.)
- In terms of *preferences*, seven out of ten colleagues chose the revised version in preference to the original when asked to judge which figure they found 'the clearer'. (This difference, while pleasing, is not statistically significant.)
- When the reading speed and factual recall measures were repeated in a *replication* study with a further 20 students, the results were almost exactly the same.

This composite picture allows me to suggest that the revised version is easier to read, that the students extract more information per unit of time, and that judges are more likely to prefer the revised version.

Case-history 4. Testing text: An iterative approach
This last case-history is introduced to suggest that in order to assess the effectiveness of one (or more) particular variables in text design, it is necessary to run a series of experiments with built-in replications and extensions. In this study Waller (1984) described how he and his colleagues at the Open University set about improving a form that was to be used by unemployed people claiming supplementary benefit in the UK.

A prototype form was developed and piloted by the Department of Health and Social Security. The form was small in format (165 × 204 mm) with eight pages organized as a folded concertina. Although the respondents found the form attractive to look at, they found it difficult to use. About 75 per cent of the forms were completed unsatisfactorily in one way or another. This meant that the forms had to be returned and/or respondents followed up in some way before an assessment of benefit could be made: a very expensive procedure.

The main sources of error in the prototype form appeared to be:

1. Problems of relevance and contextual interpretation: the form did not elicit enough information for an assessment to be made, and appeared irrelevant to a large number of claimants.
2. Problems of reading sequence: many sections did not apply to many claimants, but the form gave inadequate directions concerning which parts were to be completed.
3. Problems in graphic design: poor design practice also contributed to the problems of sequencing.

The problems of the form ranged from the fairly obvious to the subtle and the debatable. In order to redesign the form a prototype was first tested with small groups of appropriate respondents. (Interestingly, part of this assessment included the use of an eye-movement recorder to assess which pieces of text were read and in what order.) The aim of this first assessment was to isolate the main causes of difficulty, and to collect data against which the redesigned forms could be compared. It appeared from this first testing that the form was not asking the right questions to gather the information that the civil servants needed. In addition, many questions were ambiguous.

Thus a redesigned version was prepared with the emphasis on revising the language and the sequencing of the form: the content was well spaced and simply designed so that the confusions brought about by poor design practice (noted earlier) could be avoided at this stage. The revisions focused on making the branching instructions more explicit, and on giving users clearer instructions when they encountered one.

This redesigned version was then evaluated (again with small groups of appropriate respondents). It was clear that improvements had been made, but that more could be done. So a third version was prepared. Headings for the different sections were added, and the routing instructions were further improved. The testing of this third version showed that this had solved most of the problems. A fourth and final version was then prepared. Now that the logical and linguistic problems had been sorted out, the typographic detailing could be enhanced. This version used colour coding for the main headings (earlier versions had been in black and white), a larger page-size (200 x 330mm) and yet another re-sequenced order.

This final version was tested with larger groups of appropriate respondents. The results now indicated that about 75 per cent of the forms were completed satisfactorily (as opposed to the original 25 per cent). Today, after further revisions, the successful completion rate is estimated to be over 80 per cent. These impressive results have led to massive cost benefits for the Department of Health and Social Security.

Concluding comments on the case-histories
Many methods of evaluating text are limited in one way or another. It is rare to assess complete texts, and most studies have limitations.
None the less, I maintain that testing in a limited way is better than not testing at all – for the reasons given earlier. The results provide us with information which accumulates and which we may (or may not) be able to capitalize on in subsequent decision making.

Summary

1. The contents of instructional materials can be checked for accuracy, bias, etc. by using rating scales and checklists.
2. The layout and technical quality of a text can be assessed with the checklist provided in this book.
3. The suitability of a text for its intended readership can be assessed by several measures: different methods suit different objectives, but a combination of measures is likely to be more useful than one measure alone.
4. The case-histories presented in this chapter indicate the value of the methods of text design advocated in this book.

References

Bainbridge, L (1990) 'Verbal protocol analysis', in Wilson, J R and Corlett, E N (eds) *Evaluation of Human Work*, London: Taylor & Francis.
Britton, B K, Gulgoz, S and Glynn, S (1993) 'Impact of good and poor writing on learners: research and theory', in Britton, B K, Woodward, A and Binkley, M (eds) *Learning from Textbooks*, Hillsdale, NJ: Erlbaum.
Farr, R and Tulley, M A (1985) 'Do adoption committees perpetuate mediocre textbooks?', *Phi Delta Kappan*, 66, 7, 467–71.

Klare, G R (1976) 'Judging readability', *Instructional Science*, 5, 1, 55–61.

Reid, D J, Briggs, N and Beveridge, M (1983) 'The effect of pictures upon the readability of a school science topic', *British Journal of Educational Psychology*, 53, 327–35.

Taylor, W L (1953) 'Cloze procedure: a new tool for measuring readability', *Journalism Quarterly*, 30, 415–33.

Waller, R (1984) 'Designing a government form: a case history', *Information Design Journal*, 4, 36–57.

Suggested further reading

Berghahn, V R and Schissler, H (eds) (1987) *Perceptions of History: An analysis of school texts*, Oxford: Berg.

Chall, J S and Conard, S S (1991) *Should Textbooks Challenge Students? The case for easier or harder books*, New York: Teachers College Press.

Davison, A and Green, G (eds) (1987) *Linguistic Complexity and Text Comprehension: A re-examination of readability with alternative views*, Hillsdale, NJ: Erlbaum.

Hartley, J (1994) 'Is this chapter any use? Methods for evaluating text', in Wilson, J R and Corlett, E N (eds) *Evaluation of Human Work*, 2nd edn, London: Taylor & Francis.

Landauer, T K (1988) 'Research methods in human-computer interaction', in Helander, M (ed.) *Handbook of Human-Computer Interaction*, Amsterdam: Elsevier.

Rye, J (1982) *Cloze Procedure and the Teaching of Reading*, London: Heinemann Educational.

Schriver, K A (1989) 'Evaluating text quality: the continuum from text-focused to reader-focused methods', *IEEE Transactions on Professional Communication*, 32, 4, 238–55.

Sims-Knight, J E (1992) 'To picture or not to picture – how to decide', *Visible Language*, 26, 3 and 4, 324–87.

Wright, P (1985) 'Is evaluation a myth? Assessing text assessment procedures', in Jonassen, D (ed.) *The Technology of Text, Vol. 2*, Englewood Cliffs, NJ: Educational Technology Publications.

Wright, P (1988) 'Issues of content and presentation in document design', in Helander, M (ed.) *Handbook of Human-Computer Interaction*, Amsterdam: Elsevier.

Zimet, S G (1976) *Print and Prejudice*, Hodder & Stoughton.

Postscript – Designing text for busy readers

▼

Text for busy readers needs to be short, clear and action-oriented.

▲

Busy readers do not have time to read most of what is sent to them.
Writers, therefore, need to provide a summary of the key points.
A good maxim to follow is to supply 'one page of A4'.
The summary should be clearly laid out, so that the essential points can be mastered quickly.
The summary should conclude with clear recommendations.

▼

Summary of the book

In this text I have argued that writers need to consider:

- the purpose of the text
- the readers of the text
- the spacing of the text
- the wording of the text, and
- the instructional contribution of additional facilities such as graphs, tables, diagrams and colour.

I recommend that people buy it, read it, and implement its suggestions!

Subject Index

Author Index